Local Sources
for the
Young Historian

Local Sources
for the
Young Historian

Robert Dunning

FREDERICK MULLER

First published in Great Britain in 1973 by
Frederick Muller Limited, London NW2

Copyright © Robert Dunning, 1973

Printed and bound in Great Britain by
Morrison & Gibb Limited, London and Edinburgh

ISBN 0 584 62045 4

For Anne

Contents

List of Plates

Between pages 50 and 51

List of Maps

Preface

This book is for the beginner in the study of local history who is looking for material near at hand and comparatively easy to use. There is really no end to the sources from which the histories of our towns and villages can be studied and written, but there is a limit to the amount of time that can be spent during leisure hours, at weekends or during holidays. So the number of sources dealt with in this book has been deliberately limited; they have been chosen to give a fair coverage from early times to the present day, and to demonstrate that an important part of local studies involves working out of doors, looking at buildings, following roads, tracing the courses of streams and hedges.

Readers and users of this book may well find that some chapters and topics interest them more than others. Apart from the first two chapters, which are closely linked together for obvious reasons, each subsequent chapter deals with a separate topic which can be treated alone. Suggestions for further study included after each chapter are intended to give guidance to those who wish to pursue any subject in greater detail.

The history of the parish of Wilton, Somerset, which forms the second section of this book, is included to demonstrate how much can be drawn from the sources this book describes.

Acknowledgements

For permission to quote from records in their custody I am indebted to the Rev. Prebendary Roland Clark, vicar of Wilton, and to the Rev. Michael Wynes, rector of Berkley and Rodden. Mr. Ivor Collis, County Archivist of Somerset, not only allowed reproduction of material in his custody but also gave generously of his time to read much of this book at an earlier stage. Thanks are also due to Mr. H. L. M. Patten, Secretary of the Somerset Archaeological Society, for permitting the reproduction of material in the Society's collections, and to Mr. K. A. Horne and Mr. R. C. Sansome for providing illustrations. I am most grateful to Mr. Joseph Thomason who is responsible for the plates, and to Messrs. A. J. Warren and R. J. L. Cooney for drawing the maps.

I am indebted to the vicar of Wilton for permission to reproduce plates 2, 3, 5 and 13; to the Somerset Archaeological Society for plates 1, 10–12; to the Somerset Record Office for plates 6, 7; to the Somerset County Museum for plate 15; and to Cinquorme Photos., Taunton, for plate 16.

Introduction

A book on sources must begin with some kind of instruction as to where such sources are to be found. In the chapters which follow references are made to County Record Office, Parish Chest and Local Library, so we must be clear what these places or collections of documents are, for until you know where to find the sources, all the knowledge in the world about them will be of little value. So if you have decided to study the history of a town or village, or of a canal or a road, the first thing to do is to make the right choice.

Naturally you will want to choose a place you know, either the village where you live or the parish where your school or college is. This is usually a good idea because you will probably know where old lanes are, where interesting houses can be found, and who are the people who can best help with memories of the place as it used to be. But it is quite possible that the sources for this particular place have been lost or are not easy to get at. For someone who has already started work on such a place, this can be a great disappointment, and may put them off local history altogether!

So before you make your final choice, before you read too much of this book with just one parish in mind, it would be as well to write to the Archivist at the County Record Office, asking whether he has in his keeping the kind of records you are likely to be able to use. At the same time you should write to the vicar or rector of the parish, to find out what records he has in the Parish Chest or safe, and whether he will allow you to study them. If the answers from both are that records are available, then you can proceed.

The next stage is to study this book so that when you look at the parish records and the documents in the Record Office you will know what pieces of information to look for and how to use them. You should also visit your local library. The reference librarian should be able to tell you what, if anything, has been written about your parish or canal, or whatever you have chosen.

Those who wish to go into greater detail should ask to see the publications of the county or local archaeological society, which may run to over a hundred volumes covering geology, archaeology, folk-lore, history and many other topics about your district, and possibly on your particular parish. There may also be a record society covering your area, too, which will provide you with even more details from original sources.

If you want to limit yourself to the sources described in this book, the librarian may be able to show you some of the maps described in the first two chapters, and he may have pictures and old photographs as well as the directories described in Chapter VII.

When you have finished at the library, you should write to the County Record Office again to arrange a convenient time for a visit, particularly if you are going in a group. When you write, say what parish you are working on and what you have already done, and then list what you want to see, perhaps beginning with the tithe map. Which brings us to the sources themselves. . . .

All this work cannot be done in three or four afternoons, and it is best not to rush, for in your hurry you may make mistakes and often miss important clues. And you will need patience at times, for some of the documents you will at first find difficult to read. If you stick at it, however, you will soon get used to the different styles of writing and the abbreviations, which at first seem rather like a secret code.

Everyone works at a different pace; but everyone should work to some sort of pattern. It is best to decide before you start just exactly what you want to do, and stick to it. Whether your task is large or small, you will collect your material until you have so many notes you find them difficult to arrange. You remember writing something down about a house, or a canal, but you cannot find it. So try, if you can, to collect your notes so that each one has a separate piece of paper. Each sheet, say 8″ by 6″, should have at the top the name of the book or manuscript from which you took the information, together with the page number. Some notes will be used for only one topic in your history, others may be used several times, so mark each sheet with the section or sections for which you will use it. Then, when you come to write your history, you won't spend all your time looking and none writing.

PART ONE

I

Maps

THERE are maps of several kinds which every local historian will find of use when writing the history of any town or village. They may be divided into four groups:

(a) those compiled before the foundation of the Ordnance Survey in 1791;

(b) those compiled in recent years to reconstruct the landscape at different periods of history;

(c) those produced by the Ordnance Survey from about 1800 to the present day; and

(d) those compiled either officially for Enclosure or Tithe Commissioners, or privately for estate owners.

What value have maps in each group for the student of local history?

(a) Maps made before this country was accurately surveyed vary considerably in quality. One of the earliest, drawn about 1250 by a monk called Matthew Paris, shows the whole of Britain, but the shape is scarcely recognisable, and only a few places are marked, very inaccurately. Between the late sixteenth century and the early nineteenth century, a succession of map-makers produced maps of counties and of some of our larger towns, many of which can still be bought today for a few pounds. Unfortunately they are not of much use to local historians; the early ones, such as those by Christopher Saxton (died 1611), John Speed (born 1552), or Richard Blome (atlases of 1671 and 1673) do not have roads marked on them. Towns and villages are marked with standard symbols, and even hills are pictorially represented. Perhaps the only points of interest are that some, like Saxton's, show parks and forests, and some, like Speed's, often have small plans of towns in their corners. These are often the earliest town-plans we have, but are rarely very accurate, and are really too small to be of great help. But they are better than nothing.

The art of surveying improved very much towards the end of the seventeenth century, particularly in the work of John Ogilby (1600–76), who in 1675 published a careful survey of many of the main roads in the country. The maps are printed to look like strips of parchment with the course of the road upon them. Features near the roads—houses, churches, bridges, windmills, beacons and even gallows—are included wherever possible. These are the things that a traveller in the seventeenth century would see from his coach.

From this time the standard of the maps was very high; they began to show the roads more accurately, and these will enable you to plot the routes of the turnpike roads described in Chapter VI. But these maps are nearly all drawn to a small scale; they are not of much use in studying a town or village in detail. There are, however, more detailed maps of large towns, particularly for London. Your local librarian or archivist will be able to tell you about these.

(b) In recent years the Ordnance Survey has compiled maps to reconstruct the landscape as it was in times past. These are based on just the kind of material we shall be trying to get from maps ourselves, and from the fieldwork of archaeologists and historians. In particular they concentrate on finds of Roman villas and roads, on ruins of castles and monasteries, on hill forts and burial grounds. These maps, too, are on a small scale, one or two sheets covering the whole of the country. They will, however, tell you whether you live near a Roman road or a Saxon cemetery or a ruined monastery, and so help you to understand something about the background of your area before you start doing detailed work.

In this series of maps, you will find the following helpful:

  (i) *Ancient Britain* All major archaeological remains from prehistory to the Norman Conquest are shown. Two sheets.

 (ii) *Southern Britain in the Iron Age* Britain south of a line from the Isle of Man to Scarborough in the thousand years up to the coming of the Romans. Two sheets.

(iii) *Roman Britain* A.D. 43–410—towns, villas, roads, mines, potteries, signal stations. One sheet.

(iv) *Britain in the Dark Ages* From 410 to the death of Alfred. One sheet.

 (v) *Monastic Britain* The religious houses of Medieval Britain. Two sheets.

(vi) *England in the Seventeenth Century* England after the Civil War. One sheet.

There are also some maps of special areas such as Hadrian's Wall, the Celtic earthworks of Salisbury Plain, and maps of the Neolithic sites in the basin of the river Trent, in Wessex, and in South Wales.

(c) Of even greater value—indeed local historians cannot work properly without them—are the maps of the Ordnance Survey, beginning in 1801 and still being revised and reissued. The earlier ones are almost historical documents themselves, because so many of the things marked on them have changed or disappeared—new roads and towns built, railways constructed, villages and towns changed in size. The first edition of the 1″ to 1 mile maps are now being reproduced quite cheaply with local historians in mind.

The modern maps, too, must be studied, particularly if you are working on a village or town you have never yet visited. Many of the documents you will come across as you work will describe roads or rivers not by the names known today but by names such as "the road from Norton", or "the stream which runs to Southwick". So you must know where Norton and Southwick are before you can begin to look for the road and the stream. You must know where the nearest market town lies, where the nearest river is, whether the village or town is near the sea or in hilly country, for all these things will have a bearing on the history of the place. And to find out the answers you will need maps.

Maps are drawn to various scales. The 1″ to the mile maps, including those made in the early 1800s, cover, of course, a larger area on each sheet, but give fewer details. The most useful for local studies are the 2½″ and 6″ to the mile maps. Both give many more details such as field boundaries and better details about houses and roads. The larger the map, the better; you can use the large ones, provided they are your own, instead of notebooks to record the names of fields and what crops are grown in them, together with all kinds of information such as the place where you found Roman pottery, where the parish boundary follows a deep ditch or a large bank (see p. 10), or the inscription on a boundary stone.

There are even larger maps, which are best to use if you are working on a town. Some of these maps are a hundred years old, and were made after the Public Health Act was passed in 1848, to establish where wells and drains were. Some of them are very detailed indeed. I have a copy of such a map for Warwick. It marks wells, wash houses, stables, sewer grates, fire plugs, water plugs, lamp posts, privies, piggeries, dust bins (not, of course, the small ones we use today), pumps, sinks, coal bins, boilers, cisterns and dung pits! And on such a scale garden paths, summer houses, brew houses, public houses and factories are all individually marked. You can even tell which houses are made of stone and which of wood, and what the roads and footpaths were paved with. To find whether your town has such a map see *The Historian's Guide to Ordnance Survey Maps* (National Council for Social Service).

From all this information you could write a splendid description of Warwick; and if you look carefully, even the houses themselves can be "rebuilt". In one part of the town, not far from the canal and a hat factory, is a block of houses labelled "Brookhouses or Commercial Buildings". Each house is numbered, and you will find there 37 dwellings, built back to back in a long row. Numbers 26 to 43 face away from the town towards green fields, but north-west, and therefore have little sun. There is one lamp to light the alley which runs in front of these houses, at the entrance to a passage which cuts through the middle of the block, and leads to the houses facing in the other direction. Numbers 26 to 43, eighteen houses, have no sinks inside, and have to share between them six outside ones. The houses on the other side face the town, and overlook a yard with twelve sinks, four privies and nine pigsties. You only need a little imagination to picture what it was like to live there; and if you look at Warwick newspapers at the time the map was drawn, in 1851, you will discover that more than one family lived in each of these houses, and that the total number of people in the 43 houses was between two and three hundred.

Not all maps will be as informative, but it is true, you will find, that the more you look at a map, the more you will learn.

(d) The fourth group of maps contains those drawn for particular purposes, which we deal with in turn:

Estate maps   As their name implies, they are not usually maps of parishes, unless the landowner in question owned the whole of a parish. These maps are of smaller areas, sometimes manors, sometimes farms, sometimes parks or just groups of fields. If you are very lucky, you may find one dating from the end of the sixteenth century; they begin to be common from 1700 onwards, though your parish may not have such a map at all. These maps are often coloured, and are very detailed. I have seen maps such as these showing the gardens and grounds of a mansion, marking ponds, shrubs and even statues; and maps of parks with deer leaping over fences and rabbits in kitchen gardens eating lettuces. These are not official maps, so the men who drew them could allow their imagination to work overtime.

Enclosure maps Between 1760 and 1840 the farming arrangements of many parts of the country were changed. Instead of the countryside being divided neatly into fields of manageable size, many parts of England were still cultivated on the "open field" system, whereby one farmer had many strips of land scattered in various parts of the parish. There were also areas of land, known as common or waste, where several farmers, sometimes all the villagers, had the right to take their cattle to feed. This system was very common during the Middle Ages, but by the eighteenth century there was every reason to put an end to it by letting farmers gather their strips together into workable units, and dividing commons for more sensible management. Sometimes the farmers in a village agreed privately among themselves that this should be done, and got on with the job. This was all very sensible, but for the historian a disappointment, because usually nothing was written down and no map was drawn to show what the village was like before. But very often they could not agree. Everyone in Stoke under Ham, in Somerset, agreed that the old system of farming was inefficient, but the farmers there were so jealous of each other, each thinking his neighbour would get better land than himself, that the bad old ways were continued for another thirty or more years. They were brought to an end by an Act of Parliament which appointed men to draw up a plan to divide the large fields, made up of hundreds of separate strips, and map out fences and hedges; to work out how much the rights of each villager were worth in the common pastures, and to arrange compensation for them in the form of land carved out of the old fields. In order to do this, a detailed map had to be made; a map, usually, of the new arrangements, not of the old. And there is another difficulty about these maps. The Act of Parliament and the commissioners were only concerned with the lands still divided in the old-fashioned way; so their maps are usually only of such areas. Sometimes the area will be most of a parish, sometimes only a very small part. If you live in the midlands, or in other areas of late enclosure, it is quite likely that you will find maps marking these old strips, as well as land described as "ancient enclosures". Other areas, such as the south-west, are less fortunate in this respect.

These maps do not come alone—or should not. There is also an *award*, an explanation of what man was awarded what piece of land in place of his old right to take his cow to graze on the common, or of what piece he got in exchange for the piece given to his neighbour. The fields on the map are each given a number, and the award will tell you what the field was called, how large it was, who owned it before the changes and who was the new owner. So if you are lucky enough to have such a map of your village, you will have to study it closely.

Tithe maps If you do not find an enclosure map, you will probably find a tithe map. Tithes were taxes paid to each vicar or rector; they were not paid in cash, originally, but in animals, corn, hay, apples, honey, and many other things, including beer. These arrangements were probably made when the parish was first created, perhaps as long ago as the tenth century, at a time when money was scarce and farm produce was the only way a man could pay. But in more modern times paying lambs and hay to the vicar became inconvenient both to the payer and to the receiver. Some vicars made private arrangements with their parishioners so that cash instead of kind, known as a modus, was paid. The Tithe Commutation Act of 1836 finally put an end to payments in kind, and in each parish a settlement was made whereby the owner of each property agreed to give the vicar money instead of lambs or hay or whatever he had usually given. But in order to find out exactly what each should pay, a detailed map of the parish had to be drawn up, rather like that for the enclosure award but covering the whole of the parish subject to tithe payments.

Tithe was owed not only for land but often for houses and gardens, so the maps are usually on a large scale, each house being separately numbered. This means, of course, that the maps for large parishes are sometimes very big and awkward to manage; but it also means that there is enough detail to keep local historians busy for some time. And, because tithes were paid in most parishes in England, you are very likely to find such a map for your own parish, drawn at some date between about 1838 and 1854, which will form the beginning of a detailed study of the parish of your choice.

Tithe maps are really mines of information if used carefully, and are important for several reasons:

(i) they may well be the earliest map of the parish, since

enclosure maps are often limited to those parts still in common;

(ii) they show the boundaries of the "ancient parish", that is the ecclesiastical parish, the area for which the vicar or rector is responsible, rather than the area under the care of the parish council (the "civil parish"), which may be different;

(iii) like enclosure maps, tithe maps have awards attached to them: these list the names of the owners and tenants of the land and give the names of fields and descriptions of houses; these awards also show how each piece of land is cultivated.

From all this information, therefore, you can begin a detailed study of a parish. You will soon find, however, that the award is not arranged very conveniently for historians! It was not, after all, made for them, and like most other records, it has to be made to give up its clues. The award, you will find, is arranged so that the landlords come in alphabetical order, but the field numbers are all over the place. The larger the parish, of course, the more confused it all seems, and the more difficult it is to find the numbers. So I suggest you organise your attack as follows:

(i) Make a tracing of your parish, including all the field boundaries, roads and footpaths, from the first edition of the 6″ maps made by the Ordnance Survey. Even the largest parish will then be of manageable size. Then carefully compare the fields with the earlier tithe map and put in or rub out any changes, so that you have the outline of the tithe map on your own paper.

(ii) On your own map write in the numbers and names of the fields, the number taken from the tithe map, the names from the award. Now you can begin to ask yourself various questions about the parish at the time the map was drawn, and then, more difficult, to try to build up a picture of how the parish came to be like that, how the fields were cultivated, how they acquired their names. For example, ask yourself who held the largest farms in the parish, and what fields belonged to them. You might shade one farm blue and another red. Now you will see whether they are compact or whether they are scattered. Again, you may prefer to find out from the colouring already on the map whether the land was more arable, or more meadow or pasture. From your knowledge of geography you may be able to find out why. (For more research ideas see p. 22.)

The names of the fields you have on your copy of the tithe map may well give you some valuable clues about the layout of the parish, possibly much earlier than the date of the tithe map. First see whether any fields have a name followed by the word "field", such as East Field or Great Field. You may find several fields with names alike and guess, therefore, that these small pieces were once part of a very large field, divided into many strips each one held by different people. These were not divided by hedges, just by banks of earth. When they were ploughed, some had furrows one way, some another, and groups of strips in one of these fields might be called a furlong. So perhaps you will find a field called East Field Furlong. Not all fields will fit into a pattern like this, but a beginning has been made. When you are able to visit these fields or when you see aerial photographs of the area, look carefully at East Field Furlong, or whatever it is called, to see if there are any traces of the old furrows and ridges.

You may, of course, live in a part of England which either never had such large fields in the first place, or lost them very quickly. But still there will be something to tell from the names of the fields. Quite recently, when a motorway was about to be built through Gloucestershire and Somerset, a search was made of all the tithe maps along the route. From the names of the fields the remains of two Roman roads and the sites of Roman buildings were found. Fields called "castle" probably didn't have castles in them, but almost certainly once had ruins of some kind, which may well turn out to be Roman. "Lost" villages, villages left by their inhabitants because of plague or poverty, or destroyed by a landlord because he wanted to keep sheep there or because the village spoilt his view, can also be found from tithe maps. A field called "Town Field", miles away from any village, may very well be the site of one of these.

Not all fields have such things under them, but their names can still be amusing and helpful for the local historian. In the next chapter you will find how a deer park was found through a study of field names. A name like "Gallows Four Acres" shows the site where many a highwayman or sheepstealer has been hanged; "Snake Furlong", next to some woods, was no doubt so called because adders and grass snakes from the wood were to be found there; and "Beaton's Leaze" was certainly once held by a Mr. Beaton. But you must take care, too, not to jump to conclusions. A field called "Brandy Cisterns" in Ilchester, in Somerset, sounds as if it were a series of tanks of liquor instead of meadowland, six hundred years earlier measured in areas of a sixth of an acre, a sester. The brandy part is still a puzzle. And not far away, at Stoke under Ham, you will find on the tithe map an area called Holy Field, bounded by Holy Lane and Prophet's Lane, and a tree, which is still there, called Holy Tree. Local historians had theories about the tree being a place of pilgrimage and a preaching place. Fortunately there is an earlier estate map which answers the problem. Only fifty years earlier than the tithe map the field and lane were called Holloway Field and Holloway Lane. The field was called after the lane which is hollowed out of sandstone. So take care not to let your imagination run away with you. These field names were hardly ever written down, but learnt simply by sound. Find out the names of the fields today and compare them with those of your tithe map. For certain you will find changes. To be safe, search any other local records you can find before you construct your theories.

The fields on your map will be very irregular in shape, like a jigsaw puzzle. In some parts of the country which used to be covered in forest, such as parts of Shropshire or Sussex, fields seem to fan out from the village, those farthest away being shaped as if someone has carved them out with a swinging motion— which is just what happened; for they were cut out of woodland as more and more land was needed to grow corn and feed animals. In other parts of the country the parishes are long and narrow, some parts on high ground suitable for ploughing, the rest on marshy ground or by streams to provide grazing and water. If water is very far away, some parishes are even in two or more parts.

Look again at those field shapes. Some hedges are quite straight, probably measured out when the land was enclosed; other hedges follow streams or old tracks. Some grow on huge banks which may be the boundaries of a Saxon estate (see p. 10); some fields are surrounded not by hedges but by stone walls. But even hedges need investigating: it may now be possible to estimate the age of a hedge by counting the number of different kinds of shrubs, each kind representing a hundred years of life. You will probably have to learn some botany first, but then who knows what you may discover about the early history of your parish, and about how and why it was divided into the fields we know today. And that is just what the local historian has to do.

II

Maps on the Ground

EVEN the most experienced map-reader often gets the wrong idea of a place by looking only at maps, and many local historians have tried unsuccessfully to write about places they have never visited. As soon as you can, go and visit the parish or village for yourself, go and explore that part of your town you have chosen to study in detail. You will probably need several days to do the job properly, for there is much to look for. One of the first tasks in dealing with a country parish, and sometimes the most difficult, is to follow the boundary of the parish as it was when the tithe map was drawn. This will probably mean a walk of several miles, so perhaps the best way is to do it in stages.

Before you begin on the boundaries, however, try to discover whether there is a Saxon charter relating to your parish which gives boundaries. Sometimes you can still trace them on the ground, and they may even coincide with the boundaries on the tithe map. Here is part of a typical Saxon charter, giving the boundaries of Ilminster, in Somerset, in the year 725:

First eastwards to the head of Chalkwell (well=spring); thence west to Catshaw (shaw=wood), thence by the wyrtrum (=tree root or edge of wood) to the long linch; thence to the Dowlish (a river), thence by the wyrtruma to Cressford; from Cressford to the White Way; thence by the wyrtruma to the stickle (=steep) path; thence to Stouberninge; from Stouberninge to Dunna's gate; thence to Dunna's pool; thence to Dunna's grove; thence to the red thorn; thence to the slap (?=slope); thence to the Ethyn ford; thence by the bank to the rough (=rich, woody) lea; thence to Caducbourn; to the stream; thence to Man's Worthy (=farm), thence to Dyke valley, forth to the stream to where Ashwell flows into the Ile; thence to the brook to the landbrook to the stream, to the head of Chalkwell.

This particular charter is a forgery, so the experts tell us, but it is still valuable, for it gives the boundary of Ilminster at least at the time of the forgery in the twelfth century, if not before. Now

10

what do you notice about that charter? The boundaries, as in most Saxon charters, are given clockwise, and many of the marks are natural features, woods, a path, streams or a valley. Sometimes boundary stones or trees are mentioned. So most of these, except of course the trees, are features we may hope to find today, if we know where to look. The names, too, may be of help: you may think it would be impossible to find Dunna's gate, the gap near the farm owned by a Saxon called Dunna; but there is a village next to Ilminster named Donyatt, which is the same word as Dunna's gate.

So we must first discover whether there is a Saxon charter with a description of the boundaries. Your librarian will be able to help you here. If there is one of your parish, you may find that someone has gone before you, and has worked out the Saxon boundaries on a modern map. Even if this is the case, it is worth studying further, for at least one of the scholars who printed and published these charters hardly ever stirred from his library. The result is that other people who later actually walked the boundaries have found mistakes, sometimes very bad ones.

When you have found your charter and either checked or plotted the old boundary, compare it with the tithe map, entering those features you are sure of, and indicating others which are less certain. You will then have the beginnings of your town or village on paper: the ground plan of your parish, within which to put, in your imagination or with some certainty, the outline of the open fields to be traced from the enclosure and tithe maps, or from other sources, as described in Chapter I.

If you do not have a Saxon charter to follow, you still have the boundary from the tithe map, a boundary which may well be as ancient as many Saxon charters. The map would have been drawn in the nineteenth century, but the boundary may have hardly changed in a thousand years or more. Look carefully where it runs: not often across a field, but along a hedge or a lane, or following a stream or wood. There may, indeed, be a pathway running along the edge of the parish, in some places known as a Procession Way, the route taken every year by the villagers to "beat the bounds" of the parish (see p. 54). Sometimes these Procession Ways are still marked with boundary stones, on which are carved a cross or the initial letters of the parishes on either side of the boundary line. These stones are often marked on the larger scale Ordnance Survey maps with the letters B.S. for

Boundary Stone. Even in towns they are still to be seen on walls or on the edges of pavements; there is one, for example, in Tottenham Court Road, London, just outside Heal's, formerly on the edge of the pavement.

You will probably be able to trace the "Procession Way" for a short distance, either as a "green way", an often overgrown or muddy lane, or as a footpath now running along the edge of a field. You may also find it mentioned in field names, but here you should be careful. In the village of Stoke under Ham, some distance from the parish boundary, is a field called "Procession Orchard". Obviously the procession did not pass that way; it was so called because the owner had to provide food and drink for the people taking part in the procession.

So much for boundaries. But just before we turn our attention to roads, let us ask ourselves why the parish has its particular shape? This is a question with almost as many answers as parishes, but one general answer may be that many parishes probably began as an estate held by a particular landlord. He would want on his property land for ploughing and growing corn, and also meadow and pasture land for his cattle, wood to provide building material and water to drink and to drive his mill. Domesday Book, compiled in the eleventh century, shows England divided into hundreds of estates like this, though some had only a small amount of meadow, others hardly any arable land, others again with no stream to drive the mill, depending on where the estate happened to be. Some parishes are so shaped that it seems the landowner almost stretched his boundaries in one direction or another to include some meadow, to reach a stream or to include good corn land. Some parishes, indeed, are in two or more separate pieces for the same reason.

Examples of this kind of parish can be found in many parts of the country. At the western end of Berkshire, and reaching into Wiltshire, is a series occupying the northern slopes of the Berkshire Downs overlooking the Vale of the White Horse. They are all of similar and rather peculiar shape, long and narrow—some are as much as four miles from north to south, but sometimes less than a mile from east to west. Within these parishes, the villages themselves are almost in a line, built part way up the slope of the Downs. These parishes are so arranged that each has a share of the rich, corn-growing land on the top of the chalk Downs, and also a share of the equally rich though often wet clay valley, where the lush

grass, well watered by streams and rivers, provides grazing for
cattle. The villages are all built on the "spring line", where the
water comes from the hills, providing plentiful drinking water all
the year round, and also water to drive mills.

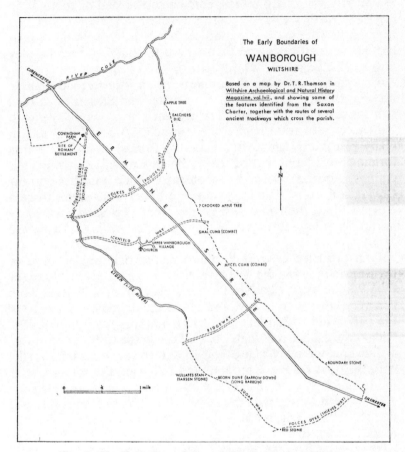

FIG. I. The Early Boundaries of Wanborough, Wiltshire

   Figure I shows Wanborough, one of these villages. There is a
Saxon charter for the parish, together with its neighbour, Little
Hinton, and a careful scholar has studied both the charter and
the parish before coming to the conclusion that the boundary as
shown on the tithe map is substantially the boundary of a Saxon
estate. Some of the Saxon boundary points are shown on the map.
Like its neighbours, Wanborough had its cornfields on the Downs

in the south, its meadows in the valley in the north, and the village in the centre, on the spring line. Its boundaries are interesting, for they follow in some places very ancient trackways, even older than the parish itself; older, therefore, than Procession Ways. You will often, indeed, come across a road or footpath in a parish which seems to ignore the village completely, and it is worth following it on a map to see where it leads. Wanborough has its share of these, and they are worth studying, because they may be like those in your own parish.

The most obvious one is Ermine Street, a Roman road running between the Roman towns of Cirencester and Silchester. It runs straight through the parish. The ancient site of the village, with the church, seems to ignore it completely. You will find this in many places throughout the country; Roman roads sometimes forming boundaries, but rarely having ancient villages along their courses. Notice the second Roman road, which branches off near Covingham Farm. The junction is the site of what seems to be a Roman town, even now being excavated. The Saxon boundary purposely follows this road for some distance, calling it *Tobrokene Strate*.

Four other tracks cross Ermine Street at right angles, three of them again ignoring the village; all four are probably much earlier than Wanborough village itself. The *Folces Dyke*, or Thieves Way, is a very ancient trackway, and forms the boundary not only of the parish but of the larger district known as the hundred. The Ridgeway, as its name suggests, runs along the top of the Downs, a wide grassy track which people have used for centuries. Parallel with this, but on lower ground, and following the spring line, is the Icknield Way, the line of a modern road which now links the villages in this area, though it seems that the road came first and that the villages began where they did because of people using the road. Finally, there is the Rogues Way, called *Folkes Dic* in the Saxon charter. This ran along the valley, and was probably not passable in wet weather. It was used until not much more than a century ago by drovers taking cattle to London from the West of England.

These five roads, Ermine Street and the four tracks, were there before the Saxon estate was carved out of the countryside, before Wanborough existed and became a parish. Wanborough's boundaries, like Ilminster's on page 10, are largely natural, following valleys, rivers or streams; marked by stones, some of which are still there, crooked apple trees and thorns which are certainly not. The people of Wanborough wanted good corn land, good meadow and pasture; if the roads that were already there were in convenient places they would use them, if not they would make their own tracks to reach their fields and farms.

So much for roads and boundaries. Something has already been said about shapes and names of fields; this is a huge subject, about which several books could be written. As an example of what can be done by combining work on maps with work in the field, let me tell you of a small discovery I made some time ago. I was studying the tithe map of Kingstone, a small parish quite near Ilminster, in Somerset. I had begun by looking at the names of the fields, to see whether there was any trace of the old "open fields" with strips owned by various farmers mixed together, which was the common method of farming in many parts of England in the Middle Ages and later. Sure enough, there were fields called West Field or Western Field and Ludney Field; and there were others called Metforland, Woolverland and Delverland which earlier had been spelt Metefurlong, Wulfurlong and Delfurlong, the word furlong meaning a group of strips arranged in one of the "open fields". And then I noticed that several fields included the word "park" in their names: there was Lower Park and Higher Park, Higher and Middle Park, The Park, and Part of the Park. What did this mean?

It certainly did not mean the kind of park we find in many towns today, neatly laid out with lawns and flower beds. But it might mean part of the grounds of a large country house, planted with avenues of trees, and provided with an ornamental lake. Yet there was no trace of such a house in Kingstone, so it was not likely to have been that sort of park. The alternative was a much older kind, an area where deer and other wild animals were kept, sometimes for hunting, but more often simply for food. The laws of England forbade anyone to have such a park without the king's permission, and so we know about many of these deer parks because we have copies of the king's letters; but no such letter has been found for this park. So I had made a discovery; but this is not the end of the story. I still had to find the park itself on the ground.

You will remember that the fields in a tithe map are each numbered, and that in the document called the tithe award all the fields and other properties are listed according to the name of the owner. So I had to collect all the fields with "park" as part of their names, and then find them on the map. When this was done (see fig. II) I had a rough idea where the park was. Now in order to keep deer and other animals safely, something better than a

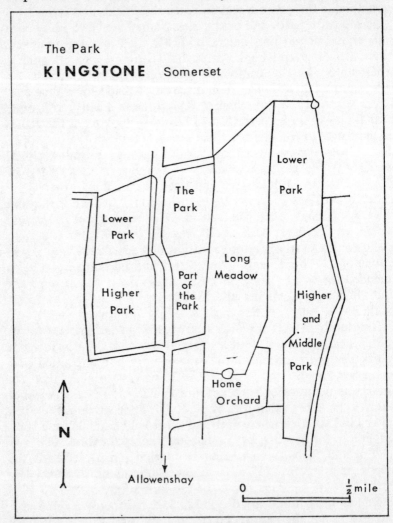

FIG. II. The Park, Kingstone, Somerset

hedge had to be devised, and the usual method was to dig a deep ditch and thereby create a high bank, on top of which a wooden fence would have been set up. Even the most agile deer would then have difficulty in escaping but equally, deer from outside

might be encouraged to come in. So the next step in the search
was to see whether there were still signs of a large ditch and/or
a high bank along the hedgerows around the edges of what I
thought was the park boundary. They were both there, the ditch
more than six feet wide in places, the bank some ten feet high.
With a tithe map of the nineteenth century I had found a deer
park dating back to the Middle Ages.

Having looked at boundaries, roads and fields, let us turn to
rivers and streams, or rather to what we associate with them,
bridges and mills. Bridges, whether large ones taking main roads,
or small ones taking farm tracks, are well worth studying. Very
few of them have date stones or anything useful like that, and
some will be so overgrown that you will need to cut down brambles
or stinging nettles to find them. There are still some so narrow
that only a single man or horse can cross at a time; these are often
called packhorse bridges, bridges which take tracks that were once
important trade routes from one part of the country to another.

Almost every parish which had a stream or river had at least one
water mill for grinding corn. Some of these mills may still be
working today, others may have been turned into private houses.
Very often there have been mills on the same site since the time
of the Domesday Survey in about 1087, though you will not
make the mistake of thinking that the same building still exists.
Bridges and mills may well be studied together, from the point of
view not of the parish, but of the stream or river. I know of one
very valuable study like this: the author, equipped with a notebook
and a camera, walked the length of a small river, noting and
describing all the bridges which crossed it, all the mills of various
kinds which drew their power from it, and many other buildings
which were associated in some way with it. His completed work,
bound in two folders and well illustrated with phtoographs,
deserves to stand as a model for other local historians.

The study of a river is a large undertaking, so begin with a few
bridges and one or two mills. Treat the mill buildings as you
would a house, as described in Chapter IV. Note carefully the
condition of the mill, how the water was diverted from the main
stream into a race or pond, how its flow was controlled by sluice
gates, how it passed by or under the mill and rejoined the main
stream. These facts you may well not be able easily to find on the
ground, and you will have to go back to the tithe or other old
maps for the clues and answers. Let me give you an example of

how field work and maps together helped me to rediscover some mills and their workings.

A modern map will show you that the river Yeo divides the town of Ilchester in Somerset from the parish of Northover. The river is crossed here by two bridges. The larger, which carries the main road, has been there for about 750 years, though it has been widened at least once, and at first glance looks modern. The centre of this bridge rests on a small island, on which a small prison was built, on one side of the bridge, and a chapel on the other. The second bridge, known as Pillbridge, is more than a mile downstream. It is very narrow, and appears now only to take a farm track across the river. Pillbridge, however, is also rather a high bridge, high enough for a boat to pass underneath. But why have a bridge there if only a farm track was involved?

The next stage in this piece of research was to find an earlier map, and as usual the tithe map was the best. The Ilchester tithe map marked both bridges clearly, but did not add much to what I already knew. But the track, which now connects Pillbridge with the town, seems to have been of some importance a little over a hundred years ago. The tithe maps also showed two mills on the river, one just outside Ilchester, upstream of the main bridge, the other in Northover, not by the main river at all, but worked by a man-made stream running behind the gardens of houses in Northover's main street. And there was one other point to note: a piece of land just below the main bridge, was called "Coal Wharf".

Still, therefore, there were questions unanswered. Pillbridge was constructed with a high arch to allow boats to come upstream to the coal wharf. But did other boats stop at Pillbridge and was the lane leading to the bridge once more important than a farm track? What has become of the two mills? Part of the answer came from an earlier map, this time a sketch map, dated 1776. It showed a group of buildings by Pillbridge. With the help of some other documents once belonging to the Corporation of Ilchester, it was possible to get a little further, and to discover that this group of buildings included a warehouse, and that there used to be houses at intervals along the lane.

The last stage of the enquiry was to visit the site, to see Pillbridge and the two mills. Pillbridge is still there, crossed now only by sheep, but built to carry packhorses taking goods from one village or town to another by the most direct route; but there are no traces of any buildings, either along the lane or near the bridge, except for a cattle shed with a chimney—obviously once a private house. There is, however, something which the maps could not show. Just downstream from the bridge are the remains of a wharf, the side of the river being embanked with large stones. There is even a large ring for tying up boats. Smaller boats could sail under the arch and proceed to the coal wharf beside the large bridge nearer the town; the larger ones had to discharge their cargoes at Pillbridge, where they were stored in the now vanished warehouse, or taken by packhorse to the town or neighbourhood.

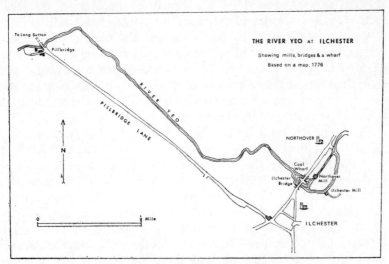

FIG. III. The River Yeo at Ilchester

And what of the mills? Northover mill is still there, now a private house, but the mill-stream has been filled in. As for Ilchester mill, I had to have a tracing from the tithe map to make quite sure where it was! It has almost completely disappeared, only a few worked stones at the river's edge being left to tell the tale. The mill race, by which water was brought across two fields, has been so carefully filled in as to be impossible to follow. It is difficult to believe that it was grinding corn only a hundred years ago.

Boundaries and roads are going to be met with in every parish without exception; rivers, mills and streams in most. There are also other features marked on modern Ordnance Survey maps which will be of interest to the local historian, and there may be others which have not, like the park at Kingstone, so far been

L.S.—2

noted, and which will have to be found out through careful examination. Not all, or indeed many, of these can be mentioned here, but one or two of the most common are worth a few words of comment.

The first of these features are castle mounds, usually marked on modern maps, though occasionally confused with burial mounds. Some of these mounds are quite small, and it is difficult to imagine how they could once have been castles; others are so large as to appear almost like natural features: for these reasons, such castles are still being discovered. The most recent discovery is at Glastonbury, found as the result of excavation by local archaeologists. Castles of this kind were introduced into Britain in the eleventh century by the Normans. The mound was usually a high, round, steep-sided one of earth, surmounted by a stone or wooden tower. The mound often overlooked a courtyard, itself defended by an earthen bank, called a bailey. It was joined to the mound or motte by a drawbridge. The lord's quarters would have been in the motte, those of his men in the bailey.

These castles, built by the Normans during the conquest, are to be found near important roads or fords. A large number of very small castles of this kind were also built during the civil war in the reign of King Stephen (1135–54), often illegally by men who took advantage of the war to rob their neighbours: these castles are often called "adulterine" castles, and most were demolished— or at least the towers and walls were demolished—by King Henry II after Stephen's death. The motte and bailey castles still to be seen today as mounds were therefore those which Henry II demolished, or others which for different reasons ceased to be military strongholds. They are now frequently difficult to find, some distance away from towns or villages, often hidden in woods.

In clay country, lowland areas and river valleys you will find sites marked on Ordnance Survey maps as moats. These are ditches, either wet or dry, enclosing rectangular platforms. In some parts of the country, particularly in Eastern England, nearly every parish has one of these moats, and sometimes as many as six or more. Near each moat you may well find other banks and ditches. The moat itself once surrounded a farmhouse and other buildings, serving as a defence against men and animals, and as drainage for the house and a place to keep fish. The banks and ditches were probably enclosures for farm animals, for gardens, meadows and crops. These moats, remember, were once in open country, still wild and inhospitable, and it was very necessary to protect crops and animals from deer, wolves and human raiders.

Sometimes with early documents, more often through excavation, it is possible to date the construction of these moated sites, which in general were occupied between the twelfth and the fourteenth centuries. Like motte and bailey castles, these sites are very often covered with trees, and are the homes of badgers or rabbits; these animals are good excavators, and I have found medieval pottery at one such moat thanks to the activities of badgers.

Another feature sometimes marked on maps is the lost village which we mentioned earlier. In some parts of the country, particularly in the Midlands, large areas of land were converted from arable to grass during the period from about 1450 to 1550. This was usually because it was more profitable to raise sheep for wool than to grow corn. As a result many villages were deliberately dismantled, and villagers elsewhere lost their jobs as ploughmen and carters. Today we can still sometimes see enclosure banks which were built around the village gardens, the platforms on which the simple houses stood, and even the sunken track which was the village street. Here again rabbits and badgers, or modern ploughs may bring fragments of pottery to the surface which will give a clue to the date when the villagers left.

This chapter is called "Maps on the Ground", and in it I have suggested how you can combine work at a desk with work in the field, using maps as guides. There is another guide, indeed a kind of map in its way, which local historians ought to use more than they do. This "map" is the aerial photograph. The whole country has been photographed by the R.A.F. and the results are available; some commercial firms also can provide prints of towns and important sites. Depending on the time of year a particular photograph was taken, the angle of the sun, the height of the camera or the dryness of the summer, many features will come to light which maps will not reveal. A dry summer, when crops turn yellow if growing where the soil is shallow, or stay green where it is deep, have led archaeologists to buildings and ditches which they never dreamed of finding. A low sun or melting snow in winter time may show up the ridges and furrows of the strip system of medieval farming, or even the enclosures of a lost village which no other source has mentioned. A great deal of skill is needed to interpret these aerial photographs, but for the local historian they are of very great value, for they supplement the information given on maps, and often provide the only clues to remains both on and under the ground.

Study suggestions:
Ideas for work have been incorporated in the text of Chapters I and II, and are not repeated here. Some additional ones are:

(a) Study the enclosure awards to see what new roads were made in the parish as a result of the changes in the fields. Old roads, footpaths, bridleways, parish pounds and quarries may also be found from these enclosure and tithe maps.

(b) Compare field names from enclosure and tithe maps with modern names.

(c) Like the open arable fields, meadows were often divided into strips marked by stones. These stones are shown on the early large-scale Ordnance Survey maps. Search for any still surviving.

(d) Most parishes had a pound where stray cattle were kept. The pound is usually marked on the tithe map. Can it be seen now? What is it used for?

(e) If the bridges in your parish now carry public roads, they are probably looked after by the County Council. Ask your County Archivist for plans and other papers relating to these, and study any changes made in the bridges, especially where they have been rebuilt.

Where are the documents?
Tithe and enclosure maps and awards will be found in your County Record Office. Tithe maps and awards may also be in your local "Parish Chest". The Record Office will probably have the best collection of maps, but you would be wise to ask your librarian and also the Secretary of your County Archaeological Society. Your librarian will help with books containing Saxon charters.

III

The People of the Parish

WHEN a historian writes the story of his town or village he wants to go back in time as far as possible. Archaeology will tell him something about his chosen subject up to and including the Roman period, and even perhaps down to Saxon times. From then onwards he has to depend very much more on the written word; unfortunately, throughout the Middle Ages most of the words written were in Latin, and in a style of handwriting which takes some hours of study before it can be easily deciphered. Another difficulty is that very many of the documents we ought to study are kept in places where they are not easily or conveniently seen by people who have limited time at their disposal, even supposing they could go to London or elsewhere. Fortunately, others have thought of this problem already, and many counties have a Record Society, whose aims have been to print selections of these documents, sometimes still in Latin, sometimes in English, and always of very great value to local historians. Not all Record Societies have produced the kind of sources now to be discussed, but several have certainly done so. Your County Archaeological Society may also have published similar documents, and some others have been printed privately. Your librarian will be able to tell you exactly what has been done for your area.

These sources are only a very small part of what probably exists about your village or town; but they will help you to see that what at first appears to be a lot of difficult material can ultimately create a picture of the people of the parish.

Many of the documents used to write the history of a town or village during the Middle Ages, and often for many years later, were drawn up because someone wanted money. William the Conqueror wanted to know how much his newly-won kingdom was worth, and the result was *Domesday Book*; Richard II and Charles II wanted money to pay their debts, and the *Poll Taxes* and the *Hearth Taxes* were the results; many kings just wanted to make sure that everyone paid towards government expenditure, and *Subsidy Rolls* were drawn up. And, of course, every owner of land wanted to be sure that he was getting as much income as possible from his estates, and the accounts of their bailiffs and receivers are an absolute mine of information. Let us start with *Domesday Book*.

Domesday Book

Imagine trying to make a survey of the value of each piece of property in your village or town. If you try to write down how the land is cultivated, what animals are kept, what shops there are and so forth, you will get some idea of how *Domesday Book* was made. A survey like this would take a great deal of time today, but with the help of maps, computers and typewriters it would be within the realms of possibility. But nearly nine hundred years ago it would have been an enormous task, so exactly how did such a survey come to be made at all?

According to the *Anglo-Saxon Chronicle* under the year 1085, the idea of making a survey of the whole of England came from William the Conqueror himself. He wanted to have a detailed picture of his kingdom, and in particular of how much it was worth. The Chronicle reads thus:

> Then in Midwinter was the king at Gloucester with his Witan [Council] and held there his court five days; and afterwards the Archbishop and clergy had Synod [Meeting] three days. . . . After this had the king much thought, and very deep speech with his Witan about this land; how it was settled or with what manner of men; then sent over all England, into every Shire, his men, and caused to be made out how many hundred hides [a measure of land, 60–120 acres] were in the Shire, or what land the king himself had, and cattle within the land, or what dues he ought to have in twelve months from the Shire. Also he caused to be written how much land his Archbishop had, and his Suffragan Bishops, and his Abbots and his Earls; and—though I tell it at some length—what or how much each man had who was a holder of land in England, in land or in cattle, and how much money it were worth. So very narrowly he caused it to be searched out that there was not a single hide or a yard of land nor even—it is shame to tell though it seemed to him no shame to do—an ox, nor a cow, nor a swine was left that was not set down in his writing. And all the writings were brought to him afterwards.

Now it sounds very much as if the writer of these words did not much care for what the king was doing; perhaps he feared his taxes would go up once the king found out how much land he owned. But it is true that William wanted to know even how many cattle and pigs there were, though unfortunately for us many of the answers have not survived, and there is much dispute as to how the details should be interpreted. But the writer of the Chronicle has to give grudging respect to a man who could arrange and carry out such a survey. How exactly was it carried out?

Probably the country was divided into large areas, seven or nine is the most likely, and a group of men would be responsible for each area. These areas would in turn be divided into shires or counties, and each county into several hundreds. Men from each town and village were called to their local hundred court to answer the king's questions. When all the information had been gathered in it was arranged; the results that survive fill two fat volumes, one of 900 pages and the other of 800 pages, which together are known as *Domesday Book*. Two other similar surveys give even more detailed information, particularly for South-West England and East Anglia.

Domesday Book then, which for most counties is to be found in translation in the *Victoria County Histories*, will almost certainly give you some information about your town or village, and even sometimes about what are today remote farms, as they were around 1087. Towns of today, of course, were not always towns in the eleventh century; this is how Birmingham is described:

> From William son of Asculf Ricoard holds four hides in Bermingeham. There is land for 6 ploughs. In demesne is one and there are five villeins and four bordars with two ploughs. Woodland half a league long and two furlongs broad. It was and is worth 20 shillings. Ulwin held it freely T.R.E.

You would hardly recognise in this description the great modern industrial city of today. It was a small village, with under 500 acres of cultivated land (a hide measures up to 120 acres), then held by a man called Ricoard, who was the tenant of William son of Asculf. Ricoard himself had a farm there, perhaps where he lived, which in the survey is called the demesne. One plough was enough to cultivate it. But there were other small farmers in Birmingham, at least nine others, in fact, called villeins and bordars. They shared two ploughs to cultivate their land. This means that there were three ploughs in use, although there was enough land for six. We may guess, therefore, that land belonging to the village was not

in use at that time, or perhaps used for grazing cattle. We know
little of what Birmingham looked like: there was a large wood
where the villagers no doubt drove their pigs, but we don't know
how many villagers there were, what crops they grew, or what
animals they kept. We know, however, that the estate was worth
20 shillings. The last sentence tells us that a man called Ulwin
used to own the land in the time of King Edward the Confessor
(*Tempore Regis Edwardi*) (1042–66).

This is a fairly typical extract from *Domesday Book*; it only
tells a little about each estate, though some places have more
interesting information about a church or a priest, or rents paid
in bars of iron or numbers of eels. And if you live in East Anglia
or South-West England, you will find lists of animals found on
each estate, cows, pigs, sheep, horses and the rest.

Now let us go forward in time to some more obvious tax returns.
Some of these are known as *subsidy rolls*, some as *poll tax* returns,
depending on the type of tax involved. Roughly, these are lists of
people, arranged by villages and towns, who were liable to pay
tax, together with the amount of tax to be paid. Sometimes it was a
tax on land or houses, sometimes on moveable goods, sometimes, as
in poll taxes, on "heads"—that is on everyone above a certain age.
An important series of subsidy rolls has survived for many
counties from the year 1327; they are arranged county by county
and village by village, and comprise the names of the more
prosperous villagers who were required to pay. The return for
the village of Curry Mallet, in Somerset, runs as follows:

> Cory Malet:
> De Hugone Pointz xs. iiijd.
> Willelmo le Cat   xijd.
> Johanne Gernoun   ,,
> Waltero in le Hurne   ,,
> Richardo Gernoun   ,,
> Roberto de Mertok   ,,
> Nicholao Doleman   ,,
> Johanne le Bedal   ,,
> Roberto le White   ,,
> Willelmo le White   viijd.
> Johanne de Mertok   xijd.
> Willelmo Ryg   ,,
>
> Summa xxᵉ villate predicte, xxjs.

At first all this may seem not very helpful: twelve names, followed by sums of money, the whole totalling 21s., which was to be paid by the most prosperous villagers. But look more closely at the surnames to see whether they can tell us something. Robert and John "de Mertok", or "of Martock" seem to have acquired their surname because of the village from which they or their ancestors came, a village not very far from Curry Mallet. John "le Bedal" or "the Beadle", was the man who kept order in the parish, something like the village constable. Walter "in the Hurne" or "Hern", probably had a house and land in a corner of the parish which projected into a neighbouring parish, or in some oddly-shaped piece of land, for that is what "Hern" means. Robert and William le White came from a family of serfs, people who were like slaves, having a small piece of land on which to live, but having to spend much of the working week on the lord's farm, working for him without wages. And who was the lord of Curry Mallet? Obviously Hugh Pointz, who paid nearly half the taxable value of the place.

Much of this has to be guesswork. You may find, perhaps, a family name in one of these tax lists which comes up again in a later return, but most likely not. You can certainly compare the total value of the tax paid by several villages, and see which is the most prosperous; and then see whether it stays the most prosperous over a period of time. And if not, try and find out why it changed.

Better than subsidy rolls, which were only interested in the richer folk, are *poll taxes*, which were interested in all over the age of sixteen years. Unfortunately they have not survived for all villages and towns, and some have only survived with statistics rather than names. They are still very valuable for the information they give about population, but the names and occupations, where they survive, are of the utmost importance to the local historian. The tax from Bath, for which a list of payers was drawn up in 1377, tells us more about that town during the Middle Ages than all the other sources put together, for it is, like rate books (which will be dealt with later), arranged street by street; so we know how many streets there were and what they were called. And the payers' names are followed by their occupations; so we know a great deal about trade and industry in the city, and where particular traders and craftsmen lived.

As you might expect, there were more labourers (118) at this time than any other occupation in Bath. The next most popular description is "artificer", or craftsman, not a very helpful word, but from the business of a large section of the population, we may assume that at least some of these craftsmen were engaged in the cloth or wool trades. The "filators" or spinners come next on the list, and below them workers in jobs closely allied with cloth and wool: weavers, dyers and tailors, as well as merchants and pedlars. And, of course, there were those traders that were to be found in every large town: cobblers, brewers, butchers, bakers, smiths, skinners and tanners.

And which was the best street to live in? Bynburi Street had eight labourers and a tailor, "By Bathe Street" thirteen labourers, Westgate Street twelve labourers, two cobblers, a spinner and a weaver. Perhaps Broad Street, outside the city walls, on the road leading to the Cotswolds where the wool came from, was the most prosperous: fifteen labourers, seven craftsmen, two spinners, a weaver and a cobbler. At first sight this looks no better than the others, but we can guess some of the people were better off because of the large number of servants. The mayor, John Natton, lived in this street, and he had two servants; Mayor Natton paid the largest single amount of tax in the city, ten shillings.

Do not build up too many hopes about finding your village or town mentioned in poll tax returns, because only a few have been printed. But if you have them, make the most of them.

We will now jump to the seventeenth century, to a totally different kind of tax, a tax on hearths or fireplaces, and known as a *Hearth Tax*. Many more documents about these have survived, and many more have been printed, than have those already discussed. The tax was paid on all domestic hearths unless the owners were so poor as to be excused the local church and poor rates. The tax lists give the name of the householder, the number of hearths in his house, and comments as to any changes made since the tax was levied six months previously. So let us return to Curry Mallet in 1664–5:

John Pyne, 16 hearths; now Thomas Weaver have one whoe is not
   rated to Church nor poore by reason of his povertie. . . .
Jeremie Mead, 2 hearths; returned one too many by mistake. . . .
Richard Perke, 2 hearths; he hath pulled downe one. . . .

Altogether, apart from Mr. Pyne's large house with 16 hearths, there were 49 houses in the village liable to tax, three with five hearths, eight with four, six with three, twenty-five with two, and seven with only one. The number of hearths tells us, of course, something about the size of the houses; half the houses in the village had only two hearths, so no question of fires in bedrooms, and probably only two rooms and a kitchen downstairs, though the bread oven there would not be counted. It may be possible, particularly in the case of a large house, to find an inventory (see Chapter IV) of the owner's goods, which will describe the furniture and other goods he possessed room by room. The inventory and the hearth tax return together may help you to find the actual house.

The comments after many of the entries in the Hearth Tax returns tell us more about the tax, but also about the tax payers, and about the village or town in question: "he hath stopped up one" is very often found after the name of a man who would put up with the cold rather than pay such an unpopular tax; "one is only a smith's forge" tells us something of the owner's trade. "One converted to a stable" or "the house fallen down", if coming too often, suggests that the place concerned had seen better days, that people were leaving their homes, presumably because there was no work. And sometimes there are comments about the taxpayer himself: "the house void [empty] the owner gone out of the country [probably the district, not abroad]", or "Richard Collier, 3 hearths; shuts his door and refuses entrance for the half year at Michaelmas 1665". And who can blame him?

These sources—Domesday Book, subsidy, poll and hearth tax returns—have shown us glimpses of the people who lived in our villages and towns (at least the richer ones) from the fourteenth to the seventeenth centuries. Can we find any more about these people? Certainly, but the task will become very much more complicated. For some places practically nothing else exists to help us in such a search, but for many others there are such documents as court rolls, account rolls, surveys and rentals which experts have to translate from Latin and then explain before they make any sense. Your Record Office will help you here if you want to go further.

For the seventeenth century there is more which can be done with less difficulty. It has been suggested that you may try to link the Hearth Tax returns with inventories in an attempt to build up a clearer picture of houses in your parish. You can take this a step further by tracing the owners of the house in the parish register, assuming, of course, that it survives (see Chapter V). If you have an inventory, it will be dated, so you will have some idea of the date of death. Your search in the burial register should not take long. With the inventory there should be a will, mentioning, in all probability, a wife, sons and daughters. They, too, may well be found in the registers. You are then well on the way to writing a small part of the history of a family, which you can trace backwards and forwards in time, linking it with other inventories and other houses. In this way you will be really getting to know the people of the parish.

Where are the documents?
The Domesday entry for your parish will almost certainly be found in the *Victoria County History* for your county. This will be in your local reference library. Subsidy returns and Hearth Tax records may have been published by your county Record Society or privately. Ask your librarian. Very few Poll Tax returns have yet been printed, but your archivist may know of a typescript copy.

IV
Houses, Farms and Factories

PERHAPS the most important task for the local historian is the study of ordinary buildings, and especially houses, for only by knowing something about the homes of people can we begin to discover anything about the way they lived. Although few people realise it, the materials for making such a study are very plentiful. Most villages have only one church, most small towns only two or three; but most villages have a hundred or more houses, most towns several thousand—plenty of material to work on.

First let us look at the problem. Look in the window of any estate agent and you will see advertisements of houses for sale, some very modern, perhaps a few very old ones, and many in between. The modern ones, with two or three bedrooms, are probably of "open-plan", meaning that on the ground floor there is one large room, either a kitchen-diner or a lounge-diner. In addition, one house may have a separate lounge, the other a separate kitchen, and both may have an entrance hall. Not long ago, someone made the remark that these open-planned houses reflected the kind of lives most of us lived, or rather the way many of us eat our meals. Eating used to be a serious business which lasted for several hours at a time, and was the best opportunity to exercise the art of conversation. A special room, therefore, was set aside for the purpose. Today we eat either in the kitchen or in the lounge, with television or wireless turned on, and the meal lasts only a short time; we don't need a separate room, and the modern open-plan fashion reflects this.

Perhaps your house is older, and has instead separate rooms, the dining-room and the drawing-room (or more commonly sitting room or front room). The name drawing-room is important: it was originally the *with*drawing room, the room where the ladies retired after dinner, leaving the men to drink port and talk business. This was common practice in the larger houses in the eighteenth and nineteenth centuries, and lesser folk thought they

31

would like to copy the idea of having two rooms, one as a place to eat, the other a place to sit and entertain friends. But this idea, as you see, is itself not very old; and indeed, the open-plan is very much older. For hundreds of years the main room in houses both large and small served as dining-room and drawing-room, often combined with bedroom and kitchen as well.

This room is usually called the hall: not an entrance hall, but very often the only room the house possessed, open to the roof, where a hole let out the smoke from the fire. Apart from this "open hall" there may have been a separate kitchen and out-houses. These were the kind of houses, built usually of wood and plaster, in which most people in this country lived. Gradually, of course, fashion changed. People wanted to have separate rooms to entertain away from the rest of the family, so a room, often known as the parlour, was added to the hall. A bedroom might be built over this for the adults, while the children still slept in the hall with the servants. Then more comfort and privacy were needed, so they put floors across their halls, providing bedrooms for all the family, including the servants, who usually slept in lofts over the kitchen or the dairy. These alterations meant that a proper chimney had to be built, and then a staircase, often curving around the chimney. The chimney was often very large, rising from a huge fireplace which was large enough to allow hams to hang in the wood-smoke for curing, and to have seats so that the family could keep warm. And so, gradually, the houses came to look very much like those we live in today.

All this is a very general outline. These changes took place earlier in some parts of the country than in others, partly depending on what building materials were available. Remote cottages and farmhouses would have changed later than houses in towns; in some places, where stone is plentiful but the houses small, open halls are not very often found. They are quite common where houses were built with wooden frames filled with plaster or wattle and daub (wood hurdles and mud). Each part of the country has some differences of building style, and the local historian should always look out for these. The most important thing to remember and realise, however, is that despite the differences these houses have many things in common. Very many houses in our villages, and to a lesser extent our towns, though often much changed, have been standing for three hundred years and more. How do we find these, and what do we look for?

From outside, houses can be very deceptive, for until the recent craze for living in old cottages, people liked to keep up with the current fashion. In 1694 there was a serious fire in the town of Warwick, where most of the houses were built with timber frames. The wind drove the fire through several streets, and even the stone church was partly burnt because, it is said, people took their smouldering furniture there for safety. Very quickly the houses were rebuilt not, this time, of wood, but of stone, and all in the latest fashion. People in other parts of the town then became rather jealous, and many of them altered their own houses by taking down the old timber fronts and building on new stone ones, with the new style windows and doors and decorations. If you go to Warwick today you will think that the whole of the main street was built at the same time; but quite recently an expert has examined the houses and found the old timbers still there behind the more recent fronts.

When these houses were being studied, one house in particular caused interest. You can see the date 1856 on the rainwater heads at the front of the house, which itself has a modern-looking timber and plaster front. It seems that the owner at that date wanted to change the front put there after the fire in 1694, and to make the house look more as it did when it was first built. But when our expert came to examine the inside of the house he found that part of it dated from the fourteenth century, and some of the rest had been an open hall, built in the fifteenth century.

To learn such things about houses, cottages, and even out-buildings you have to consult an expert, who will have to search for clues over every inch of the house, particularly studying the roof. Few people will let you wander all over their homes. But perhaps near your home or school there is an empty house or cottage, or a barn or other farm building, that you could more easily examine. In a town you may often find a warehouse or old factory. If the building is safe, and if you have the owner's permission, you can then make a start with a survey, a measured plan of each floor of the building.

Let us assume you have found a cottage, and have the owner's permission to examine it. The first thing is to make an accurate plan, properly measured. Even from the plan you may discover something. Not long ago I heard of a lady who bought a cottage and made a plan of the rooms. She was very puzzled to find that the wall between the living-room and the kitchen seemed to be about eight feet thick, and she thought at first her measurements must be wrong. She then examined the wall, and by tapping it found that parts seemed to be hollow. In this wall was a fireplace which she did not like, and when a builder removed it he discovered a large stone fireplace, almost a small room, with seats each side of the space for the fire, and hooks dangling from the chimney which had once been used to hang the hams while they were being cured in the smoke. The opening into the room was about six feet wide and five feet high, the top made from one huge piece of stone. You cannot hope to be as lucky as this every time, but many people have found blocked-up doorways and bread ovens in their cottages. I know of one lady who discovered that her cottage had once been a chapel; behind some flaking plaster she found a carved window and two small openings, like arrow slits in castles, to allow the priest to see up and down the road.

No doubt while you are measuring you will notice other things of interest, particularly if the house is derelict. Plaster falling from the walls will allow you to see how the house is built; you may find some old wallpaper, or odd drawings, or perhaps old pieces of furniture. If the building was once a factory there may be old machines lying about.

A house which had once been a hotel and was later a grocer's shop, was being pulled down in Taunton some time ago. On the ground floor all appeared quite normal and reasonably modern, but upstairs there were many things of interest. There were, for example, many advertisements for groceries, perhaps as much as fifty years old; there was some old wallpaper, stuck on canvas, dating from the days when the building was a hotel; and strangest of all were several small tea-chests, flattened and nailed to the walls. These were gaily coloured and decorated with Chinese characters, birds and animals and human figures. Some of the boxes had the dates 1886 and 1887, and the statement that the contents, evidently China tea, had been brought through the Suez Canal. This is a far cry from local history, but it told a great deal about the use to which that building had been put.

You now have your plan; if it is a house you will have labelled the parts you recognise, such as the kitchen and the entrance hall. Now make a careful note of what the house is made of, whether wood or stone or brick; whether its roof is tiled or thatched. Look carefully for a date, sometimes to be found on the front wall, sometimes at the top of the drainpipes at the rainwater head. If you have a camera you can make a record of many features; if not, make a sketch or two of windows, doorways and other features of note. Perhaps your building is not a house but a barn, or an old mill or a factory. There are still parts worth recording even in a building which appears to be empty; make a sketch of the way the barn roof is built, or of any old machinery lying around the factory or of how the water is made to feed the mill.

Finally make quite clear on your sketch the following points:
1. The name of the house, barn or whatever the building;
2. The place, including the map reference;
3. The date you made the sketch or took the photograph.

You should make sure that on your sketch you have included some surrounding features, such as the river or stream at the mill, any other buildings near the house or cottage, and farm buildings near the barn, together with roads and footpaths. Also don't forget to put in the points of the compass.

Another important point to remember about houses, particularly if you are interested in the suburbs of a town, is their position. Townsmen, who had earlier preferred to live in or very near their shops, during the sixteenth and seventeenth centuries began to move away as they became prosperous. Some went to live right in the country, where they had invested their money in land. Others simply moved to the outskirts of towns, where it was a little quieter, removed from the bustle of the town centre. On their chosen spots they built houses, usually surrounded by large gardens to give them privacy. These houses, in most towns dating from the late eighteenth and early nineteenth centuries, can still be recognised, not so much by their style as because they are often much larger than their newer neighbours, and are still surrounded by large gardens. Many of these houses have now been converted into flats or offices, and their gardens divided to form plots for smaller and more modern dwellings.

You can get so far by studying the buildings themselves, but sooner or later you will need to look at maps and other documents to answer some of your questions. You must not expect to find a document which gives all the answers; history isn't like that. But there are some sources, already described in this book, which will be of great help—maps. Let us assume that you have found an empty building which looks as if it might have been a factory. Now find the building on the early large-scale Ordnance Survey map. This will tell you: (1) that the building was there at the date of the map (which is given on each sheet), and (2) probably the name of the building. Now go further in time and look at the tithe map. If it is there, the same two results can be achieved, but in addition you will know by looking at the tithe award who owned the building and who occupied it. If you use local Directories (see p. 66) you may be able to fill in the gap between the dates of the tithe map and the Ordnance map by finding the names of other owners.

But the job may not be as easy as that. I know someone who began to study rather like this, and found several mills which were described on maps as brass mills. Several were in ruins, and there were old pieces of machinery lying about the buildings which seemed very difficult to explain. The buildings themselves were rather complicated; and it seemed impossible to say what each part was used for, or how the remaining pieces ofmachinery worked. But this local historian did not leave the matter there; she began asking questions locally and finally discovered an old man who had worked in one of the mills as a boy. He was able to explain the pieces of machinery and the different parts of the various buildings, and his memories of working in these brass mills have now been preserved on tape.

This may well be something you have to do. Don't be afraid to ask questions; you will be surprised how pleased people will be to help you, and old folks are very fond of telling tales about the days when they were children.

The study of maps applies equally to houses and to farm buildings; from them you may be able to trace the growth of a farmyard complex, by showing how extra sheds for cows or machinery have been built. You can then begin to ask why; your answers may be that one farmer was keen on cattle, while another grew more corn. A modern farmer needs large sheds for his modern machinery; a century ago cowsheds probably took most space in the farmyard. And now there are dutch barns for baled hay and straw, where before would have been an open yard for ricks. So a study of farm buildings can become a study of how farming has changed in the past hundred years. And here again, talking to a retired farm worker will help a great deal.

There is another way to study private houses, but one which must be used with care. When a householder died, it used to be necessary to make a list of all his goods, such as furniture, clothes, pots and pans and farm stock. Those who drew up these lists, or *inventories* as they are called, often did so by going from one room to another in the house, and simply jotting down what was in each. If a room was empty, of course there would be nothing to write, but at least some of the inventories you will find at your local Record Office will tell you something about the house of the man in question.

Let us now look at three such inventories. As you will see, they are in English, but some of the worlds may be unfamiliar. Apart from finding out from them something about the houses these goods were in, we can begin to get an idea of the kind of furniture used. As it happens, these three inventories relate to one small hamlet, Longbridge, just outside Warwick. Some of the houses are still there, and from these documents it has been possible to say which was which. These particular houses are built of timber frames filled with brick and plaster.

Inventory I (from Worcester County Record Office, 1561/68c)

An Inventory of the goodes and cattalles which were Robert Boyes of Longebryge in the paryshe of Saynte Maries of Warwike who decessed the xiijth daye of Februarii in the yere of our lorde god 1559

Fyrst the haule a theale bord one payre of tresselles one forme one paynted clothe and an ambre valued or priced at	ijs.
Itm xv payre of hempton sheates priced at	xvs.
Itm iij table clothes of hempe and one hempton tooel	iijs. viijd.
Itm ij mattresses one bolster and ij twelly clothes	vjs. viijd.
Itm ij cofferes one paynted clothe and a tester	iijs.
Itm ij pottes ij pannes and a kettell viij peces of pewter a chafyng dysshe and a laver	xiiijs.
Itm iiij oxen iij kyne one mare a wayne and a plowghe with all belongethe therto	ix.li.
Itm iij stores pygges	vs.
Itm hys Raiment or apparell	iijs. viijd.

. . . total xi.li. xijs. viijd.

Robert Boyes's house seems to have been a small one; his goods were worth only £11 12s. 8d., £9 of which came from his farm stock of four oxen, used for pulling his plough, three cows, a mare and a waggon. Only one room, a hall (*haule*), is mentioned, though the phrase "First, the hall", suggests that the man who made the inventory was going to mention others and then for some reason did not do so. But Mr. Boyes certainly had very little furniture: in the hall only a trestle table, a bench, a painted cloth to hang on the wall and a cupboard, worth altogether only two shillings. He had fifteen sheets, each worth a shilling, three table cloths and a towel. And then came two mattresses, a bolster and two cloths, two coffers, a painted cloth and a tester (usually material forming a kind of canopy over a "four-poster" bed). Whether this furniture, which we would normally associate with a bedroom, was also found in the hall, or whether there was a separate bedroom we cannot tell for certain, though judging by the smallness of the total value of the goods, it seems more likely that Mr. Boyes and his family lived, ate and slept in one large room, which may have had a separate kitchen attached at the back.

Robert Boyes was evidently a small-holder. He had four oxen for ploughing, three cows, a mare, and three pigs. Bartholomew Smalley, his neighbour, was somewhat better off. He died a few months later than Robert Boyes, and his possessions were listed as follows:

Inventory II (Worcester Record Office 1560/196)

The Halle: Itm a table, a forme, a carpett, a banker, an ambery, a chayre and iiij quysshyns — vijs. iiijd.

Itm a fyre shovell a peire of tongues, a peyre of Balloes, the pot hengles with the peynted clothes in the halle — iijs. viijd.

The over chamber: Itm a standyng bedde with a fetherbedde, ij bolsters, ij pilloes, a peire of blankettes, a coveryng, a tester with the appertenaunces — xxs.

Item ij jackettes, ij dooblettes, iiij shirtes, ij peyre of hoes, a gowne, a cloke and ij cappes — xls.

The nether chamber: Itm a flocke bedde, ij bolsters, a peyre of blankettes, a coveryng with thappurtenaunces — xiijs. iiijd.

Itm iiij cofers, vij peyre of shetes, iij table clothes, ij towelles, and vj napkyns — xxvjs. viijd.

Itm in *the servauntes chambre* ij mattres, ij bolsters and ij twelly clothes — vs. ivd.

The kechyn: Itm iij brasse pottes, iij lytell panes, iiij kettels, a scommer, a frying pane, a gryd yron and a peyre of pott hokes at — xxvjs. viijd.

Itm a bason with a ewre, vj platters, vj pewter dysches, iiij sawcers, a chafyng dyshe with other smale implementes — xiijs. iiijd.

Itm a peire of cobbardes, ij spyttes with treene dyches and
trenchers   iijs. iiijd.
The Backe howse: Itm a knedyng trowe, a boltyng whithe a moldyng
bourde, a stryke with the strykeles, a kylne heare, an axe, a
hachett with other instrumentes of husholde   vjs. viijd.
Itm in breade, corne, and malte by estimacion iiij quarter, and
corne in the felde   vij li.
Cattell: Itm viij bullockes, a wayne with yowkes, tewes, with other
instruments of husbandrye   xij li.
Itm fyve kyne ij steeres ij yerelyng cawfes and iij store swyne
                                                                    vj li. vjs. viijd.
Itm a hackney nagge a sadell brydell with bootes and spurres
                                                                       xxiijs. iiijd.
Itm shepe lxvij and wood in the yarde   x li. xvjs. viijd.

Summa totalis xlv li. xixs. viijd.

From this inventory let us extract information to answer three
questions:
    1. What was Bartholomew Smalley's house like?
    2. What occupation did Bartholomew follow?
    3. How prosperous was he?
    1. Six rooms in the house are mentioned, of which five—the hall,
the kitchen, the servants' room, and the upper and lower chambers
—were probably in the main block, with the bakehouse behind. We
know that this house was in Warwickshire, and was probably constructed of timber framing, the spaces filled with brick or plaster.
    2. Bartholomew Smalley was clearly a farmer, owning six oxen
for ploughing, five cows, two steers, two calves, three store pigs
and 67 sheep, together with a waggon. The inventory does not,
of course, tell us how much land he had, but you could guess
about fifty acres.
    3. He was quite prosperous. He kept two servants—at least,
there were two mattresses in the special room set aside for them.
There was bedding in both upper and lower chambers, so the
upper was probably for himself and his wife, the lower for his
family. From this it appears that the Smalleys lived by day in the
large hall, still open to the roof. They had not thought it necessary,
or perhaps could not afford, to put in a floor above the hall to
make bedrooms throughout the house. Bartholomew Smalley had
a hackney nag, a sturdy horse to carry him into Warwick market,
overtaking Robert Boyes on the way, trudging up the hill carrying
his eggs and poultry for sale.

Inventory III is much longer. It lists the goods of Humphrey Staunton, who died in 1616. Mr. Staunton lived near Boyes and Smalley, but in a very much larger house. The inventory mentions the following rooms:

> Hall
> Parlour
> Chamber over the kitchen
> Loft over the kitchen chamber
> Chamber over the parlour
> Chamber over the hall
> Maids' chamber
> Little chamber
> Chamber over the dairy
> Men's chamber
> Kitchen
> Bakehouse.

Only a small part of this house is still standing, so it is not possible to be sure exactly how the rooms were arranged, but notice that there were three storeys in some parts of the house—kitchen, with a chamber above it and a loft above that. Secondly, here is a good example of how an inventory fails to list all the rooms in and around the house—the dairy is only mentioned in passing as being under another room. Thirdly, this house, as might be expected of a large one, had followed the fashion—the hall was no longer open to the roof; a floor had been built across the space, thus forming a first-floor room the length of the hall below. This made Humphrey Staunton's house much more like our own than Robert Boyes's or Bartholomew Smalley's.

We have used these inventories principally to find what rooms were mentioned in houses, but it is clear that we can also learn a great deal about furniture, and household goods such as cooking utensils. Many inventories are not helpful in our study of houses, because whoever drew them up did not bother to note rooms at all. Probably the goods of the former owner were collected in one place; this was certainly easier than going from room to room or creeping about in the attics and servants' quarters. Such inventories will not, therefore, be of much use in showing how the house was arranged. Even so, we can learn from the contents something about the trade or occupation of the dead person, perhaps something about his financial status, and about his furniture.

This is typical of local history sources, for they can be used in many different ways, provided you ask enough questions.

Study suggestions

Suggestions have been incorporated within the body of this chapter, combining field work "on site", measuring, drawing, sketching or photographing buildings (ranging from barns and mills to small cottages or even shops), with work on documents, such as tithe and other maps, and inventories. You might take your studies further by:

(a) finding out more about the furniture mentioned in the inventories either from your local museum or from photographs obtained from the Victoria and Albert Museum or the Geffrye Museum, both in London;

(b) collecting dialect words from local inventories, and tracing their use;

(c) collecting information about agricultural implements (photographs of these can be obtained from the Museum of English Rural Life at Reading) and about other trades in your locality;

(d) comparing the layouts of farms from a group of tithe maps for several parishes, and show how they have changed because of modern farming methods.

Where are the documents?

Tithe maps and other large-scale maps will be found in your local Record Office (see p. 22). There too you will probably find enough inventories to be getting on with. The County Archivist will advise you about others.

V

The Parish Church

IN most towns and villages, by far the oldest building is the church. Some churches appear at first to be very dull, as well as very dark, and you may think that only experts can learn anything from them. This is partly true; someone with expert knowledge will be able to tell you a great many things you would otherwise miss, so if such a person is available you would be wise to get in touch with him. But if you look carefully you should be able to find a great many things of interest.

Let us start not with the church itself but with the churchyard. Have you ever looked carefully at gravestones? The oldest you will find probably date from the eighteenth century, but you may be lucky enough to find one or two earlier. Our ancestors had strange ways of remembering their dead; sometimes the tombstones have verses as well as names and dates, and some of these verses are very crude. Gravestones are usually single slabs of stone, but early ones may take the form of huge chests, called "table tombs". In old pictures of churches, you will often see these tombstones being used as tables or find people sitting on them. In some parts of the country slate and not stone is used to mark graves, and, very occasionally, cast iron. You may also find the odd wooden one, with the name painted on the side, shaped rather like stocks without the holes for the feet, and running the length of the grave.

The inscriptions on these stones, which may well be difficult to read at first, can tell you more than you might at first imagine about the history of your town or village. You may learn something about the local families which later can be linked with the entries in the parish registers; you may learn something about local trades and occupations; you will see examples of local craftsmanship in the carvings of cherubs and skulls; and you may catch a glimpse of humour in some of the verses.

Abbotsbury, in Dorset, is near the sea. In its churchyard are a number of tombs commemorating members of the Boatswain family, and you will easily guess that one of their ancestors got his surname from the job he did. Only local tradition and an inscription on a tombstone in the churchyard at Wanborough, in Wiltshire, remain to tell of a family of soap-makers in the village at the end of the eighteenth century. And at the same place is a memorial to a nineteenth-century miller:

> God works his wonders now and then,
> Here lies a miller, an honest man.

Millers had a bad reputation for taking more than their fair share of the flour as payment for milling each farmer's corn, so an honest miller was considered remarkable.

You will not often be so lucky as to find an inscription like this one from Saltford, not far from Bristol, but if you do, your search will certainly have been worthwhile. I was told about it by someone in the village, but it took a fair time to find, and then some time to read, for moss had begun to grow over several of the letters. There is a story which tells that Frances Flood knocked one night at the rectory door and asked for a night's lodging. The rector saw she was rather crippled and told her she could sleep in the barn. When he went to see her the next morning he found that she was suffering from some horrible disease and that both her feet had fallen off. Frances is said to have recovered and to have left Saltford on her stumps, leaving her feet buried in the churchyard. They have a tombstone all to themselves which reads:

> Stop, Reader, and a wonder see
> As strange as ere was known;
> My feet fell off from my body
> In the midst of the bone.
> I had no surgeon for my help
> But God Almighty's aid
> On whom I always will rely
> And never be afraid.
> Tho' heare beneath inter'd they lye
> Corruption for to see,
> Yet they shall live and reunite
> To all Eternity.

Frances Flood, April 1st. 1723.

Now we can't be quite sure how true this all is. It would be a good idea to look at the parish registers to see if the rector made an entry to record the burial. Perhaps it was all an April Fool's joke!

If you cannot find anything of interest among the tombstones, don't go inside yet, but have a careful look around the church walls. Look carefully on the south wall, using the weather vane to tell you which that is. This is the wall which gets most of the sun, and along this wall, particularly near doorways, you may find small sundials carved in the stone. These are called *Mass Dials*, serving to tell the priest in the Middle Ages the time of the next Mass, and telling the parishioners how late they were. Some churches have several of these, carved in the most unlikely places; some may even be upside down now, showing that the stone on which they are carved has been moved. The dials themselves are not usually "working": in most cases, all that remains is a circle with lines radiating from the centre. No shadow falls because the gnomon, the stick which was once in that hole in the centre of the circle, has rotted or been broken off. You will be able to test the dial if you place your pencil in the hole.

While you have been looking for these dials you may have spotted those strange carvings high up on the walls, where masons let their imaginations run riot as they created dragons and devils and all kinds of animals to act as waterspouts or simply as decoration. Part of the church at Tiverton, in Devon, is decorated with detailed carvings of ships, because the man who provided the money for the building was a prosperous merchant whose wealth came from overseas trade.

Now go inside. There are often so many things to look at it is difficult to know where to start, and you may well need several visits to see everything, so concentrate on a few things only. But first, walk around the church trying to make a plan of the whole building. This may be very easy in the case of a small village church, or rather difficult if it is the parish church of a large town. A sketch plan will do at first, showing the different parts of the church—the nave, chancel, aisles, tower, porch, vestries and side chapels. If the church is an ancient one, it was almost certainly built bit by bit; it probably began as a small stone or wooden chapel, with only a chancel and nave. As the village or town grew, more room would have been needed to hold the congregation, so the old nave would be pulled down and made longer, or an aisle added. And the then parishioners would build a tower, probably because they wanted to have a better church than the one their neighbours had in the next parish. But building fashions changed then as fashions in clothes change today, so new and larger windows, a carved screen or a painted ceiling would take the place of the outdated features put there centuries before.

In order to find out exactly when each part of your church was built, you will have to consult an expert. Perhaps there is a guide in the church which will help; if not you will have to search for a book in your library. Experts rely a great deal on the shape, size and pattern of the windows and columns to tell them when they were made, so look at them carefully, make sketches of them, and compare them with the drawings in the books you find. Some of the windows are filled with stained glass panes in memory of someone. There may be a date around the edge of the window, but this will be the date of the glass, not of the window.

Almost certainly there will be some more memorials inside the church, either on the walls for the more modern ones, or on the floor for the older ones. Don't forget to look under the carpets! Some of these memorials will be made of marble, some of stone, and perhaps a few of brass. Those on the floor will give you an opportunity to make rubbings, though you must be sure to obtain permission from the vicar or rector before you do so, and must take care not to damage anything. Memorial brasses, usually dating from the fifteenth and sixteenth centuries, give you an opportunity to study armour and costume of those times as well as adding to your knowledge of the important people of your village or town several hundred years ago. In the same way your church may have one or more tombs with life-size effigies of the dead person lying on the top. You will be able to study the costume closely, though the tombs are likely to be very much worn, and covered in carvings made by village children hundreds of years ago. You should not add to them!

While some are looking for brasses and monuments, others may find wood carvings on the pulpit, screen, or benches around the church. Some parts of England, particularly the West Country, are famous for the woodwork in their churches. The ends of the pews sometimes show men and women at work: there is a cloth-worker with shears and other tools of his trade at Spaxton, in Somerset, and not many miles away, at Bishop's Lydeard, is a carving of a windmill, complete with the miller and his horse, and birds flying between the mill's sails. Look carefully at these carvings: sometimes you will find initials, sometimes a date, often the coat of arms of the person who gave money for the bench to be made.

There are still other things to see. Make a sketch, for example, of the font, and compare the carving there with carving in the windows in the church; ask permission to see the bells; and finally climb to the top of the tower. There is no finer way of learning something new about your town or village than to look down on it.

The "Parish Chest"

We do not have to rely on the church building alone to tell us something of the history of the parish church; there will be much to learn from the parish records. If they are kept in the church they are, or should be, kept in the church safe, and you will have to ask the permission of the vicar or rector to study them. They may, on the other hand, be deposited at the County Record Office, but a letter to the vicar will be the best approach.

Years ago, before safes were invented, church records were often kept in large, wooden chests, bound strongly with iron and secured with several locks. Some of these "parish chests", as they are called, are still found in churches today, sometimes turned into collecting boxes, sometimes into stores for old hymn books and flower vases. Many of the chests are worth studying in themselves.

Among the records you will find either in the church safe or at the Record Office are parish registers. Records of christenings, marriages and burials which took place in every parish church have been kept, or should have been kept, from the sixteenth century onwards. Some of the earliest may not have survived, though it is surprising how many begin in the 1540s and 1550s. Often, you will notice, the earlier pages of these registers are in the same handwriting, each page signed at the bottom by the vicar or rector and the churchwardens. This suggests that the entries for the first few years, sometimes as many as fifty, were copied from an earlier register—and this is indeed the case, these valuable records having been copied on parchment from the older, paper register, which would not have lasted very long.

But, of course, not all registers begin in the sixteenth century; some have been lost in fires, more stolen, some even used by people to wrap up parcels. Even today these precious registers are not always kept safely, free from damp and cold.

Yet the documents are often much more interesting than they seem to be, for many clergymen wrote notes in them of various kinds, besides the bare minimum of names and dates. Many a clergyman or parish clerk added something about some of the people of the parish—how old they were, where they lived, something personal about them or their families. Some clergy, indeed, treated their registers as diaries, and you may often find "heavy snow", or "poor harvest" or "plague", among the lists of names. So, perhaps when you have become used to the writing, and the rather odd spelling, the first thing to do is to look for comments and notes like these.

These extracts are taken from the register of one parish, Berkley, near Frome in Somerset. From the seventeenth century onwards successive rectors seem to have followed a tradition of noting matters of interest about the church and people of the parish, for which local historians should be very grateful.

Baptisms

1 July 1748	Thomas Sansum, upwards of forty, baptiz'd ye day before he died.
29 July 1756	Wm. Humfry, gentleman, the father of the three young women baptiz'd the 10th October 1755, receiv'd clinick baptism being confin'd to his bed by a mortification in his foot.
12 April 1758	John, son of William and Anne Graunt, baptised privately being like to die.
5 June 1782	James Salisbury, an ingenious painter, aged 25, born of parents called Baptists.
29 June 1790	Jane, daughter of Solomon and Anne Locke, common beggars travelling in the road.
30 August 1812	Purity, son of Barrington and Charlotte Backland, gipsies.

Burials

16 May 1565	Edward Jones, being slaine att Warmister with the plucking downe of a house, was there buried.
6 February 1608	A wanderinge boy whose name was unknowen, which dyed at Standerwicke was buried.
14 August 1637	An infant daughter of Mr. John Bayley, Rector of this church, and Edith his wife, being still borne was buried.
15 August 1637	Mistress Edith Bayley, wife of Mr. John Bayley, rector of this church, and second daughter of Roger Newborough Esquire, was buried.
19 July 1638	Roger Bourne, who dyed suddenly as hee was comeing from Frome the same day was buried.
27 April 1774	George Skreene, a stranger, died by an accident on the Road.

8 April 1794	John, son of John Kemp, aged 32, who was kill'd by a fall from a scaffold at Longleat House.
16 July 1813	Thomas Pearce of Bath, aged 63. A chairman who, being deranged, wander'd from Bath on 13 July, and was found the next morning dead, and with his throat cut on Buck's Green. An inquest was taken and verdict lunacy.

Marriages

7 August 1620	Stephen Barkley and Godpreserve Burt.
25 August 1632	John Bayley, rector of this church, and Edith Newborough, second daughter of Roger Newborough esquire, married.
17 October 1748	[A marriage was celebrated] at Rodden chapel when Berkely church was shut up in order to be repaired.
21 November 1748	[Another marriage] at Rodden chapel while Berkely church was pulling down in order to be rebuilt.

These are only a few examples from one parish, but we can learn from them more than is usual, particularly about the present church itself, built, as the register shows, about 1748. And we can find out something about John Bayley, the rector, whose daughter and wife died probably on successive days in 1637. Mr. Bayley, in fact, had rather a sad time at Berkley. In 1645, as he writes in another part of the register, he was driven out of his parish for religious reasons during the Civil War. His parish clerk, too, lost his job, and from 1654 a man called a "public register" took over the duties of entering the names of those who were married and buried; but instead of noting the date children were christened during his period of office, the "public register" in Berkley, following his colleagues in other parishes, noted the date of their birth. The "public register" at Berkley was also very bad at spelling.

Later on, in the eighteenth century, Thomas Westley, the rector, found that the parish clerk had forgotten to enter names in the parish register, and himself wrote:

There are many yeares wanting by the negligence of my clarke who kept the register but neglected to register any.

Thereafter Mr. Westley made the entries himself. This is a warning to us that, although all the registers may have survived, the names of the people we are looking for may be missing because someone forgot to write them down.

Not all registers will have such interesting entries as those of the parish of Berkley, but there is still a great deal that can be done, even with what appear to be the dullest registers, to discover something about the people in the village, their families, how long they lived, what their occupations were. It may be best to begin with the more modern registers which are the easiest to read. If it is your home parish, look up the entry of your own baptism, or that of one of your friends. Nowadays families move from place to place much more than they did a hundred years ago. Probably as much as three-quarters of the families in a village in 1850 had been there for several generations, and you would very likely have found several people who had been no more than ten miles from their homes. So, if your family has not lived in the village or town for long, go back to the tithe map to see who was there in about 1840, and try from the registers to find out how long they had been there and how many generations of the family you can trace. Or perhaps you might use one of the memorials on the church wall as a starting point. Let us imagine a memorial which has the following inscription:

> Here lies the body
> of
> James Jones of this parish
> who died the
> 21st day of December 1794,
> aet. 74.
> Also of Mary his wife,
> daughter of
> Nathaniel Price who
> died 15th March 1797
> aet 72.

We know, from the memorial, when James and Mary Jones died, but just to make sure, look up the burial register for the two years:

> 1794   James Jones, watchmaker, 23rd. Dec.
> 1797   Mary Jones, widow, March 18.

Now we need to find when they were baptised. By knowing their ages (*aet.* on the memorial means 'aged') you can calculate that James was born in or about 1720, and Mary in or about 1725, so begin by looking at the baptism register for 1718 and go on until you find them. In 1725 you find:

Mary, da. of Nathaniel and Susannah Price bapt. 9 October

but there seems to be no trace of James at all. So very likely he came from another parish, perhaps quite near, or perhaps miles away, for he was, remember, a watchmaker, and he would have learned his trade as an apprentice perhaps in a town or large village some distance away.

We must, therefore, concentrate on Mary, for, as she was born and died in the same place, so perhaps she also married James Jones there. Mary could have married him when she was sixteen or so, so begin your search of the marriage register about 1741. And, as luck will have it, you find the entry of the marriage of Mary Price to James Jones of the parish of Bradford on November 12, 1754. And look carefully at the entry in the marriage register, for when the couple came to sign their names, James could write, but Mary put a cross instead.

What we have learnt we can now put down as a "family tree":

Nathaniel Price = Susannah

Mary   =   James Jones, watchmaker
born 1725   born about 1720
married 1754
died 1797   died 1794

This is a beginning. We can then proceed to find whether Mary and James had children; or we can trace Mary's family back to discover who was her grandfather; or we can go to Bradford and unearth something about James's family.

This was an imaginary example; people who trace family trees, genealogists, find they have to travel all over the country to complete their researches. The search often gets very complicated, and becomes the work of specialists. However, local historians are more concerned with the families which stayed in their village than with those that moved away. You may simply need to construct small family trees for several families where you live, in order to find out, for example, which family has lived in your street for the longest time, starting either at the present day or from the time of the tithe map.

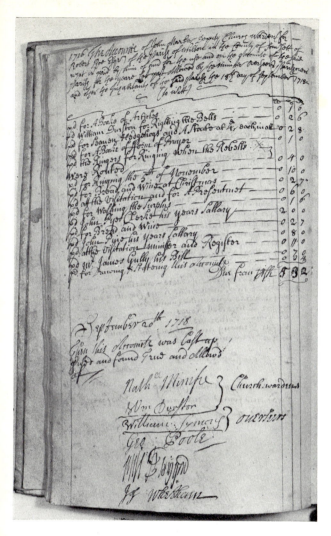

1. Accounts of the churchwardens of Wilton, 1715–16

2. Wilton church from Vivary Park; water colour by Harry Frier, 1895

3. Wilton and Sherford, 1821; part of map of Wilton parish

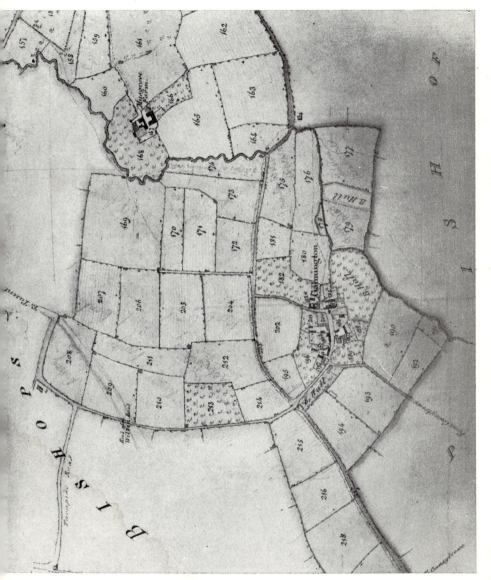

4. Galmington, 1821; part of map of Wilton parish

5. Ramshorn bridge, Galmington, 1972

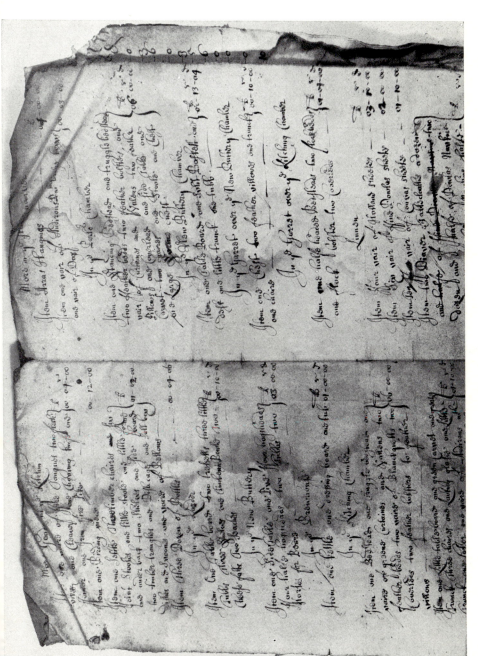

6. Part of the inventory of the goods of George Browne, 1679

A Truee and perfect Inventory of all and
singular the goods and Chattels of Ames
Blinman late of Milton in the County of Dorset
Gent deceased taken and apprised by us whose
names are hereunder written the Eight and
Twentieth day of Febru: 1688

Imprim: his Wearing apparell & money
in Purse ——————————— 08 = 06 = 00

Item In money ~~undemnified~~ due by 392 = 16 = 00
& engaged on bonds & otherwise ———
Due from Edward Swan by smalls & otherwise 68 = 00 = 00
for principall and interest about

in Plate two bread pot halfe a Guinnea two
Crown nine shilling & 8 dozen & 9 Buttons ~~ 25 = 00 = 00
Thirteen

Fourteen Paire of Sheets Canvas —— 02 = 12 = 00
and Dowlaine

Two Diaper Table cloaths and Two
Dozen of Diaper Naplins —————— 01 = 08 = 00

Fiive old Board Cloaths, & Thirteene
old Naplins —————————————— 00 = 10 = 00

~~Thirteen~~

Two Paire of Holland Pillowbers 00 = 08 = 00
Nine other Pillowties ———————— 00 = 04 = 00
Foure Towills ——————————————— 00 = 02 = 00
Foure market Cloaths ——————— 00 = 01 = 00
Twelve Yards and halfe of new Course holland 01 = 00 = 00
Two Childrens Pames and
Seaven Yards of Serge ————— 01 = 00 = 00

In the Parlour   One Bed, Bolster, Pillow and Bedsted
Chamber   two old blankets & Bedsted performed 02 = 10 = 00
One Ovall Table board, One Liverry Table 01 = 06 = 08
Six old Green chaires, One Chest, One
Trunk,
One fire Pan and Tongs, Andirons, Slice 00 = 08 = 00
& pair of Bellows ——————————

In ye Buttery   One Standing Bedsted, One Trundell
Chamber   Bedsted, Two Beds, One Blankett One
Overbed, one pair of old Curtaines & 02 = 00 = 00
Vallands, and 3 old Coffers

At the Stairs   One old Coffer and Joyntstoole 00 = 05 = 00
head

437 17 02

8. "Manor House", Galmington, 1972

9. Cutliff Farm, Wilton, 1972

10. Wilton church; watercolour by J. Buckler, 1832

11. Wilton church; watercolour drawing by W. W. Wheatley, 1848

12. Wilton church; watercolour by Thomas H. Hare, 1852

13. Wilton parish register; burials 1558–62, copied in the early seventeenth century by James Jones, curate

14. Parts of the toll board from Shuttern Toll House

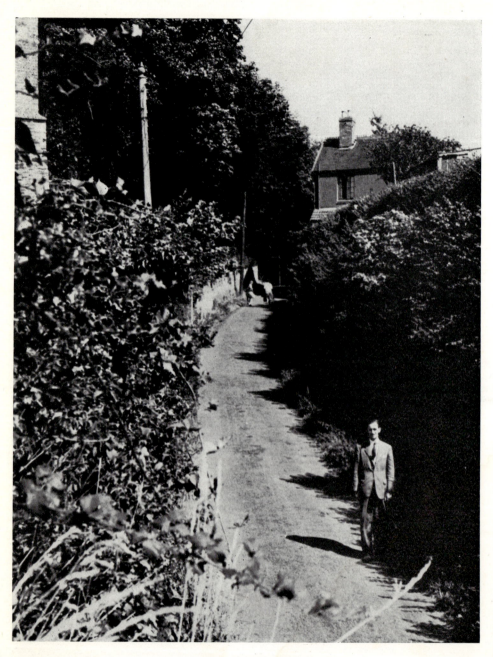

15. Toll House, Shuttern, 1972

16. Wheatleigh Toll House and Hoveland Lane (now Galmington Road), 1961

17. Haines Hill, 1972

18. Wilton Lodge, 1972

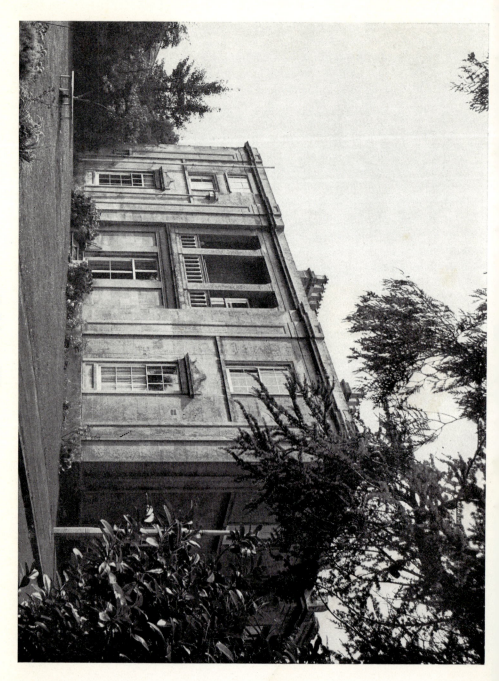

19. Belmont, 1972

Nowadays historians have become particularly interested in trying to find out about the size of families, how long people lived, and whether they moved much from village to village and town to town. It is possible, within the space of one parish, to begin to answer some of these questions as you build up small family trees like that of the Joneses. As you work through each family, you may discover something about their jobs, or the changes in fashion of Christian names, or the reason why a field or lane is called Jones's Lane or Price's Orchard, or the possibility of plague, or a cold winter when a larger number of burials than usual are entered. There is almost no end to the usefulness of parish registers.

Among the books you may find in the "parish chest" are the churchwardens' accounts, the responsibility of the churchwarden being to keep the church in good repair and generally maintain the services. These accounts often contain many other items of interest as the following, for the parish of Wilton, in Somerset, shows:

The accounte of John Marker, deputy churchwarden for Robert Roe, esquire, and Charles Bennet, deputy churchwarden for William Burcher of the parish of Wilton in the County of Somersett, of what is received and paid by them of and for the use of the said parish for the yeare last past by the Minister, parishioners and other inhabitants of the said parish the 2th day of Aprill Annoque Domini 1716 (to witt)

1714, 14th November Received of Simon Welham, esquire, late churchwarden, the ballance of his two yeares accounte
£1   5s.   10½d
Ditto received of Mr. Thomas Gunston, late churchwarden, the ballance of his accounte, allowing him 6d.   3   16   8½
Received of a church rate made 1714   12   13   11

£17   16   6

The accounte of what is paid and disbursed by the said John Marker and Charles Bennett in their said yeare for the said parish of Wilton as follow (to witt)

1714, 14th November Paid Jonathan Whetham the ballance of his accounte   8   7½

Paid widdow Hucker the ballance of her late husbands account		3	8
Paid for the booke of Articles and 4 bookes and Presentment		5	6
Paid for bread and wine 4 times		5	5
Paid for 34 hedghogs and stootes and 4 polecatts at 4d. each		14	0
Paid for ringing 29th May, King's Coronation Proclamation, 5th of November, Queen Elizabeth, the day of rejoyceing, 28th May, the 1st of August twice each day	3	7	6
Paid William Durston for 2 new wheeles and mending the bells		13	8
Paid John Pye, clarke, and John Pyne their years service	2	8	0
Paid for washing surplus three tymes		4	6
Paid att two Visitations and for two bookes	1	5	2¾
Paid for boards to mend the church railes and doors and other charges		13	8
Paid for meate, drinke, bread and other things at the Perambulation	1	13	4½
Paid for washing surplus		1	6
Paid for a hogshead of beere and other things by the orders of the parish on the kings Coronation day	1	19	0
Paid for worke done on the church porch		2	6
Paid for three bell ropes		10	4½
Paid William Pether his bill	3	1	10
Paid for drawing and stateing this accounte		3	4
Paid for drawing the rate		1	6

September 20th 1718   Totall Paid   18 3 2
Received   17 16 6

Then this accounte was cast up perused and found true and allowed of—   Due from the parish   6 8

    Nathaniel Minifie } Churchwardens
    William Durston }
    William Symons   Overseer
    George Poole
    William Bidgood
    Joseph Whetham

From this account we can deduce a number of things about Wilton church in the eighteenth century, things which were common to most churches throughout the country.

(a) *The church officials* The churchwardens, usually two appointed each year, were responsible for the repair and maintenance of the church. One or more other officers, known as overseers (William Symons at Wilton) may also be found mentioned in these accounts though usually their own accounts were kept separately. They were responsible for raising money to help the poor of the parish. Most churches also had a parish clerk and a sexton. The clerk's job was to keep order in church during services, and to attend christenings, weddings and funerals to enter up the details in the church register. For this he received a fee, of course, though as we have seen he often could not spell very well, and may not have been very careful. The clerk also attended Sunday services, sitting in a stall near the parson, and saying "Amen" at the appropriate places. His fellow the sexton was supposed to keep the churchyard tidy, and he dug the graves. The clerk at Wilton in 1714 was John Pye, and John Pyne was the sexton.

(b) *Income* The money to repair the church and pay all the other bills came from the parishioners, who paid a tax known as a church rate. Rather like the rates we pay now on property, each man paid according to the size of his house and land. The rate was drawn up each year, and someone at Wilton, probably the parish clerk, was paid 1s. 6d. for doing this. Sometimes these rates are entered in the same books as the accounts, and from them it may be possible to find out where people lived in your village or town at a particular time and what property they held. Only the very poor paid no rates, so these lists act as a kind of census of the inhabitants. If you are tracing a particular family or property, these rate books and accounts may be very helpful indeed. Notice that this year at Wilton the churchwardens overspent by 6s. 8d. This may well be because they thought they were getting so much from the rate, but afterwards found they could not collect it all; very often you will find lists of people who did not pay, as well as of those who did.

(c) *Church services* The churchwardens were not directly responsible for church services, which were the business of the rector or vicar. Each year, however, the wardens and the parson had to appear before the archdeacon, and every three years before the bishop, to report whether all was well in the parish and, if not, what was wrong. The *presentment*, as this report was called, was a form which sometimes contained a number of questions; and, as you see from the account, its compilation had to be paid for.

As for the services, bread and wine were bought only four times a year, showing how often Holy Communion was then commonly celebrated. Notice the entry concerning the surplice (surplus!), which usually belonged to the parish and not to the parson.

(d) *Church life* Church bells, you will notice, were very often an expensive item. In some ways they were like newspapers today, for they were rung not only on special days such as the Coronation day, but also to celebrate victories such as Trafalgar and Waterloo. And since they were used so much, there was very good reason why they needed constant attention. Some churchwardens paid not only money to the ringers but also beer, for ringing bells is thirsty work. Notice, too, the item above that about the bell ringers. The churchwardens at Wilton, as at many other places, played their part in keeping down pests in the neighbourhood. Hedgehogs, stoats, polecats, squirrels and sparrows are often met with in these accounts; and sometimes you will find the sexton or even a boy being paid a few pence for whipping dogs out of church during services. And, while on the subject of services again, you may sometimes find references to musical instruments. Before the middle of the nineteenth century, music in church was provided by a small orchestra rather than by an organ, and many accounts include payments for new strings for violins and 'cellos.

One other important activity at Wilton and at most other places was the annual perambulation, still carried out in some parishes today. What seems now a quaint custom once had very practical benefits, because before the days of accurate maps it was difficult to tell where your parish ended and another began. Most parishes put up crosses or marked stones (see p. 11) at particular places and then, once a year, as many people as possible went in procession from one stone or cross to another, now and again stopping to throw one of the village boys into a stream or to get two more to fight at the top of a bank, the loser being rolled down into a bed of stinging nettles. These boys would then have very good reason to remember where the boundary was should any dispute arise! Even a small parish would have quite a long boundary, so bread, meat and drink, as provided by Wilton's churchwardens, would be needed to sustain the walkers.

These are only a few of the items you may find in churchwardens' accounts. Your parish safe may well contain other things: accounts and rates of officers called "waywardens" who were responsible

for repairing roads in the parish; accounts, rates and other papers
of the overseers who found food, clothing and shelter for the poor,
put poor children out as apprentices, and ran the local poor-house.
These sources are very well worth exploring, though you would be
wise first to read W. E. Tate's book called *The Parish Chest* in
order to understand many of the documents you may find. The
churchwardens' accounts are likely to help you most in building
up a picture of life in a parish. Not every church still possesses
these accounts and papers; let us hope yours is one of the lucky
ones.

Where are the documents?

Churchwardens' accounts, parish rate books, and, of course, the
parish registers, are the property of the church concerned. Many
clergy have now transferred their manuscripts to their local
County Record Office, but it would be best to contact the rector
or vicar first, just to make sure. There may be a printed guide
available in the church. Your librarian may be able to show you
a detailed description of the building, which might, for example,
be found in one of the Penguin *Buildings of England* series, by
Professor Nikolaus Pevsner.

VI

Transport

ONE of the most rewarding subjects for local study is the history of transport. The subject covers, of course, roads and railways, but also rivers and canals and, not so often as it should, the sea. Some areas are not going to be affected by all these aspects, though roads will have to be dealt with in every parish, and most areas will have railways or rivers as well. As you study an individual road or railway, you will realise that you are beginning to get to grips with something wider, almost the history of your chosen area from the eighteenth century onwards. You will have to learn not only about turnpike roads but about what travelled along them; not only about harbours, but why they were constructed and what commodities were shipped in and out; not only about the routes canals and railways took, but how bridges, tunnels or locks were actually constructed. And you will also discover that to study transport properly you have to travel yourself: fieldwork, photography and drawing are part of the job.

Roads

We have already dealt with roads in a general way in Chapter II, and have seen how ancient trackways and Roman roads often have an influence on the shape of our parishes. Our roads are notorious, as G. K. Chesterton wrote, for the way they twist and turn as if "the rolling English drunkard made the rolling English road". Modern traffic demands that corners be straightened, by-passes made, carriage-ways widened, and almost every day we hear of motorways or trunk roads being constructed. The result is that many of our old roads are disappearing, and records of them need to be collected before it is too late.

The best sources for our ancient roads, of course, are maps, and particularly Ogilvy's road maps and the new roads to be found on the enclosure maps mentioned in Chapter I. There is, however, one type of road, the "turnpike road", which has left a great many written records, many of which will be available at your County Record Office.

Today we pay for our roads by taxes when we license our cars, though some new bridges, such as the Severn Bridge and the Forth Road Bridge, are partly paid for by tolls charged on all who cross. From the beginning of the eighteenth century many of our main roads and some minor ones were similarly maintained, tolls being paid by almost all who travelled along them. Roads so maintained are called "turnpike roads" after the spiked bar which stretched across the road to mark the beginning or the end of a piece of road under the care of a body of men known as turnpike trustees.

Before the time of turnpikes, each parish was responsible for the upkeep of the roads within its boundaries. However, the traveller on a main road, going from one parish to another, would often find one stretch of road in reasonable repair, and another just a muddy track, where a parish was poor, or a waywarden did not do his job properly. On the whole the main roads of this country in the eighteenth century were very bad, often totally impassable in winter.

The growing importance of trade, and particularly competition from canals, suggested that some efforts should be made to repair roads on a different and more satisfactory basis. Groups of men, therefore, obtained Acts of Parliament allowing them to charge tolls on particular stretches of road in return for keeping the road in good repair. These Acts of Parliament carefully define the limits within which each turnpike trust was to act, and give details of the tolls to be charged. So you should begin with a careful study of the turnpike Act for your particular area, plotting on a modern map the exact route of the road, in case some parts have gone. Sometimes a turnpike trust took over further stretches of road, so a new Act had to be obtained describing the additional routes. Your County Record Office may also have other material about turnpike trusts, such as the minutes of the meetings of the trustees, which show how these roads were administered and may tell you when turnpike houses were built or repaired. Account books, too, may have survived.

Particularly interesting are the details of the kinds of travellers expected along the roads of your area at this time. The following details of tolls come from the Chard Turnpike Act of 1815:

For every horse, mare, gelding, or other beast drawing any coach, chariot, barouche, chaise, curricle, chair, landau, berlin, calash, hearse or other such . . . 6d.

For every horse, mare etc. drawing wagon, wain, cart, or other such (drawn by two or more horses or other beasts of draught) . . . 3d.

Any unladen beast . . . 1½d.

drove of oxen or cows . . . 10d. per score.

drove of calves, hogs, sheep or lambs . . . 5d. per score.

From 5th November to last day of February every horse drawn carriage carrying timber, trees . . . toll equal to half in addition to toll otherwise demanded.

Extra charges were made according to the width of the wheels of vehicles, but certain people could travel free:

Any horse or carriage attending members of the Royal family.

Any vehicle carrying materials to be used in the maintenance of the roads.

Any vehicle carrying manure or fertilisers, crops or other agricultural produce which was not for sale or just purchased.

Any horse engaged in farm work e.g. ploughing etc. or going to be shoed, or watered as long as they did not go for more than two miles on the turnpike road.

Any person going to his usual place of worship on a recognised day of worship; attending a funeral; or a vicar, curate, etc. going about his parochial duties. These last only in their own parish.

Any carriage conveying a prisoner or vagrant.

Any carriage carrying the mails.

Any horse etc. connected with the military in any way.

Any vehicle conveying people to the elections for Parliament.

Any vehicle which shall not pass more than 100 yards on any turnpike or only cross it. . . .

The surviving turnpike records will not only tell you about tolls, and about how they were often sold for a year or more to the highest bidder; they may also contain details about how the road itself was repaired, where the materials came from, and how much money was collected in tolls at the gates. The collectors were usually provided with a small house near the gates, the house standing right on the edge of the road, with windows often so arranged that the gate keeper could see when traffic was coming in either direction. Many of these houses are still standing, others have disappeared in road-widening schemes. They can sometimes be exactly dated by reference to the turnpike trustees' minutes, and are worth studying in themselves. If you carefully study the surviving ones in your area, you will begin to recognise them elsewhere, for they are often of similar designs in other parts of the country. Many of them are now private houses, some have been transformed into little inns or restaurants, many are just falling to ruin. At least sketch these, or better still photograph them before they finally disappear. It is often worthwhile, too, to record milestones along the route of your particular turnpike: they were probably designed by one man, and you will recognise the original ones from those which have been added later. Occasionally you may find an original signpost.

What difference did these turnpikes make? They certainly improved the standard of the roads in this country, thereby making travelling and trade very much easier and more reliable. One effect was to increase the number of coach routes in the country; these may be traced from early Directories, which at the end of town-entries list the names and destinations of the coaches and carriers coming through each week, and where and when they stopped. The entry for the little town of Ilchester in Somerset in 1822–3 runs as follows:

CARRIERS: LONDON and EXETER, Russell & Co. from the Castle Inn, every Mon. Wed. and Friday.
BRISTOL, John Timmons, from the White Horse every Tuesday.
YEOVIL, John Timmons, from the White Horse every Friday.

COACHES: LONDON, the Subscription Coaches, from the Castle Inn every day at half-past one, and half-past twelve at night.
BATH, from the Castle Inn, every day (Sunday excepted) at two.
BRISTOL, from the Old Swan, every Mon. Wed. and Fri. afternoon at one.
EXETER, from the Castle Inn, every day at two, and half-past twelve at night.
WEYMOUTH, from the Old Swan, every Tues. Thurs. and Sat. afternoons at one.

Just occasionally you may find some papers, perhaps in your County Record Office, perhaps in a collection elsewhere, which show exactly how these tolls affected travellers. Not long ago I was looking at some papers of the Hinton St. George (Somerset) Cricket Club for the years 1827–30, and among them I found three scraps in the handwriting of the club's secretary. One was a

L.S.—3*

hotel bill for six shillings for breakfast at Gullock's New Commercial Inn at Sidmouth in Devon, with other items on the back, the other two were simply bills of costs, each including cheese and beer. Each also included charges for going through toll gates. Thus one bill was:

> Sidmouth Gate 4½d.
> Honiton Ditto 6d.
> Corn, bread, cheese and beer 2 shillings.
> Honiton Gate 3d.
> Yarcombe Gate 6d.
> Snowdon Gate 6d.

From this we can picture the cricket team, probably in a wagon, going off to Sidmouth early in the morning, breakfasting in Sidmouth, giving the horse corn while they played, then coming home another way, eating bread and cheese, drinking cider, and no doubt singing, especially if they had won the game.

Railways and Canals

These are rather difficult to tackle from local sources alone if you want to study them in very great detail, since they are almost always still the property of the British Transport Commission, and as such their records are usually kept in London or York. However, your local Record Office and probably your librarian will still be able to help, and there is plenty of field work to do, trying to trace the course of a canal which has not been used for years or a railway whose track has been taken up.

When a canal or railway was planned, a detailed map of the proposed route had to be sent to the Clerk of the Peace in the county concerned, so that anyone who objected to the route suggested might do so. These plans, called "deposited plans", are now to be found in County Record Offices. It was quite possible for a new canal or railway company to collapse even before the waterway was constructed or the track laid, so you may well find a plan of a canal or railway through your parish which was never actually made! These plans, you will find, are very detailed, showing the names of owners of the land through which the proposed route was to pass, together with the tunnels, locks, lifts and stations to be constructed. Armed with a modern map on which the details from these plans have been plotted, you can begin your field work by following the route on foot, and discover, particularly in the case of canals, locks that have not been moved, lifts and tunnels that have not seen a canal boat, for years.

Nowadays railways are disappearing almost as fast as canals did sixty or seventy years ago. Weeds have grown over many tracks, but still wayside stations survive, sometimes turned into private houses; level crossing gates can still be seen permanently open to the road; one may even come across railway carriages converted into chicken houses and garden sheds. Deposited plans will certainly show you where the track lay and can lead you to an abandoned quarry or coal mine. Along the route you may find a piece of track still in place, perhaps an abandoned coal truck, or one of those cast-iron notices telling people not to let their cattle stray on the track.

The County Record Office is unlikely to have detailed records of the railway and canal companies, though it would be wise to ask, just in case. There may, however, be copies of the Acts of Parliament which set up one or more of the companies in your area, and perhaps some private correspondence between a landowner and a company about land along the route. These letters can often be extremely amusing, as some landowners were very much against such new-fangled things as canals and railways, and very unwilling to part with their property.

But if the official records of these companies are not to be found locally, your search in local newspapers, described in Chapter VII, may well reveal news items dealing with the construction of railways and canals. It is often possible to trace progress month by month until the triumphant opening day, including all the accidents which occurred. And don't forget old photographs, showing rolling stock and locomotives, if you are dealing with a railway. There may be a collection in your library, and you can often still find some old person who can remember something about the early days of a railway or the last days of a canal. I remember hearing an old lady of over eighty tell how, as a girl, she used to run down to the lock on the canal near her home when news came that a barge was there—so even at that time traffic must have been rather rare.

If you are interested in canals, you will be wise to begin by studying one of the general books on the subject by Charles Hadfield. You will find these most interesting and well illustrated, and they will help you to picture how your local canal looked in its hey-day, what goods were carried in the barges, and why, in the end, canals went out of business.

Harbours

For those who live on or near the coast, the history of sea transport is a vital part of their local history. Particularly fascinating are those tiny harbours which for one reason or another are no longer used, but which, to the careful observer, still bear traces of a busy and prosperous past. One such harbour is Portgain, on the north-western coast of Pembrokeshire. On the Ordnance Survey 1″ map it appears simply as a small village at the head of a rocky inlet, a little to the east of some extensive quarries. A visit to the village tells a very different story. There are, to begin with, a number of small cottages, typical of the area, but arranged haphazardly, with no real suggestion of a proper settlement, no clearly defined streets nor anything like a village green. And there is a harbour, overlooked on the west by curious high brick walls in front of the cliff face, broken by tunnels and square holes, and flanked by a number of other abandoned buildings. Rusty ironwork, cables, and rotten planking give a rather eery atmosphere to the whole place. Now what were all these buildings, and is there any connection with the nearby quarries?

The high brick walls in front of the cliff face in fact form giant hoppers for holding stone, brought from the quarries by overhead cars. Some of the tracks can still be seen. The square holes were the chute openings which controlled the flow of the stone from the hoppers into waiting trucks on the harbour's edge, and these in turn discharged it into the holds of ships tied up at the quay. The tunnels in the cliff face linked the quarries directly to the harbour, probably providing access for the quarrymen. The abandoned buildings nearby no doubt still bear traces of the driving machinery for the overhead railcars which kept the hoppers full of stone. All this and more could be found out by a careful examination of the site. The best find of all was made some days after I had visited Portgain; it was a group of photographs of the harbour, a sea of masts, crammed full with sailing vessels painted with the names of stone firms in Bristol and elsewhere.

The history of Portgain, or at least part of it, was thus pieced together from field work and the use of old photographs. But not all abandoned harbours reveal their history so easily. One at Lilstock, on the Somerset coast, can certainly be traced on the ground, with the masonry at the harbour mouth still in good condition. But there historians have so far come to a virtual standstill; they are not sure why it was built, when it was abandoned, or what goods came in and out. All that can be said now is that it is useless, a large bank of shingle blocking its outlet to the sea.

Portgain and Lilstock are examples of the best and the worst the local historian can hope for or fear. Another Pembrokeshire harbour, Solva, is perhaps about average. It is now a quiet anchorage for holiday-makers' yachts and dinghies, still preserving, of course, its quay and also some old lime-kilns, circular stone structures about ten or twelve feet high with an arched cavity for the fire at the bottom. If you look carefully in several of the tourist shops in the neighbourhood, you will probably find an engraving of Solva made some hundred years or more ago. The harbour is shown then full of sea-going sailing ships, many with two or three masts, trading vessels, not holiday-makers' yachts. A careful search through local newspapers, early printed histories of the county, and the papers of local landowners, now in the County Record Office, reveal that those ships were there to fetch copper, lead and silver, mined not far away; cloth, woven in several mills built in the steep valleys quite near; and lime, burnt in the kilns, and then taken for use as manure to other, less fertile, parts of the country.

A harbour still in use will prove a much bigger problem. Its records will probably be housed at the Headquarters of the local Harbour Board. Almost certainly a beginner in local history would be well advised not to tackle such a large subject.

Study suggestions

(a) Trace turnpike roads on a modern map from the original Act, and any other Acts extending the range of the trustees' activities. Compare the route with surviving earlier maps and show any changes in the course of the roads.

(b) Collect photographs and sketches of toll houses and milestones.

(c) Trace the course of a local canal from the Deposited Plan on a modern map, and then try and follow the course on foot.

(d) Similarly, do the same for any railway in your locality not now marked on modern maps, sketching or photographing any remains.

(e) Make plans of any closed harbours known to you, including any buildings connected with them.

(f) Collect references to transport from local newspapers.

(g) Use Directories and any other sources such as newspapers to show how transport in your town has changed over the last 150 years. You will probably find it served first by coaches, then by railways, and then by buses. Note the number of carriers both by road and by canal, and the growing number of garages on the roads.

Where are the sources?
Acts of Parliament for canals and railways and turnpikes will probably be found at your County Record Office or at your Reference Library. The Record Office will have other records of Turnpike Trustees, Deposited Plans for roads, railways and canals. Your library will probably have old newspapers, Directories and perhaps some old photographs.

VII

Towns and Villages in the Nineteenth Century

THE sources described in this book are, on the whole, more useful for writing the histories of villages than for town studies. On the other hand, some, such as the large-scale maps described in Chapter I (p. 3), can only be found for towns, and both tithe and enclosure maps will be useful starting points for those who want to study all or part of a town. Similarly, subsidy rolls and the entries in Domesday Book are quite as useful for town as for village histories. Some of these sources have been described in Chapter III (pp. 25–9).

In addition to these and other sources already mentioned, many towns have preserved their own records, dating perhaps from the sixteenth century, sometimes including the minutes of meetings of the governing body and perhaps also account books of the town's finances, records of town courts, of markets and of apprentices employed there. Even more towns will have preserved the charters granted to them by the Crown over the years which gave them the right to govern themselves, hold courts, and take the profits of markets and fairs. The charters will be in Latin, but translations may have been printed. Charters by themselves will show you in outline how the town's governing body increased in power over a period of several hundred years; its other records will show you, provided they survive, the details of how this power was exercised, and how the everyday business of the town was carried on. These records are usually still kept in the custody of the Town Clerks of the towns concerned; Record Offices sometimes hold the records of those small towns which in more recent times have lost their ancient rights to self-government.

You will probably very soon be swamped if your town has records surviving from the sixteenth century. They will almost certainly be difficult to read in the first place, and then difficult to understand, even though probably written in English. It will be best to start in the nineteenth century; you may well have to do so anyway if your town has, like many, lost its records either by accident or because some former Town Clerk or Mayor decided that his administration of the funds had better be forgotten. So before tackling the official records of your town, even if they survive, and of necessity if they are lost, it will be as well to see what other sources are available.

It is obvious that nothing will quite take the place of official records, but it is perfectly possible to write a balanced history of any town without them, at least for the nineteenth and twentieth centuries. Three sources in particular will be useful; two are printed, and therefore do not present the difficulties of the older records, and all are quite easily available. In order of treatment they are Commercial Directories, Newspapers, and Rate Books.

Directories
As trade between towns increased at the end of the seventeenth century, businessmen needed to know where to find people to buy or sell their goods in other places. The first such Directory is a list made in 1677 of London merchants, but not until the end of the eighteenth century are they found in any numbers. Only in the nineteenth century are these directories of any great value to the local historian, to the extent that the historian of any town will not be able to get far without them.

It must always be remembered that these early Directories were published for commercial reasons, to allow contact between buyer and seller, very much like the yellow pages in our modern telephone directories. For this reason only certain types of information are given, arranged in a particular way. The local historian has therefore to sort out what he wants, often by simple analysis. The most important thing for the original user of the Directory was to know the names, occupations and addresses of the most important people in any town or village. He would want to know how the town was governed, who the Mayor and the Town Clerk were, and the names of the leading clergy and gentry. The town's institutions, such as schools or libraries, and its lines of communication by coach, canal, river and later railway would all be necessary information for the man thinking of opening a factory or a shop, or widening his market. Most Directories of towns also provide some sort of historical sketch; this can often be very misleading and inaccurate except for contemporary events. For these it may be the only source.

Now let us look carefully at a typical early Directory, to see the kind of information which may be expected. One of the best of its kind is William West's *History, Topography and Directory of Warwickshire*, published in 1830. As its title suggests, it is something more than a simple commercial directory, but the kind of information it contains is usually to be found in other Directories of the period. Let us take, for example, the entry for the county town, Warwick. The entry begins with six pages outlining the history of the town and its castle, with very valuable information about the town as it was at the time the Directory was published: this includes details, which have not been found elsewhere, about factories. There follows a list of members of the Corporation, the county officials, the Members of Parliament for the various parts of the county, and other information of that kind. Then come the names of the nobility and gentry of the town and neighbourhood, and an alphabetical list of the more prosperous businessmen, with their trades and occupations, and the streets where they lived. After these names are details of local banks, the address of the Post Office and the hospital, the number, names and stopping places of the coaches coming through the town, with the times of the arrival and departure, and the road and canal carriers with their agents, including the frequency of their journeys to the villages of the neighbourhood and beyond.

The next Directory for Warwickshire was published twenty years later, by Francis White. This is arranged slightly differently, but provides much the same kind of information. One new feature is a "list of Streets, Roads, Lanes, Squares, Terraces, &c. in Warwick and its vicinity", which, when compared with the streets named in the earlier Directory show how the town had grown in the interval. After this list come the nobility, clergy and gentry, together with the names of partners in business houses. Then comes the list of business people, this time not arranged in alphabetical order, but under various occupations. These can sometimes be amusing, such as John Spicer, who was described as a "Bird and Animal Preserver and artificial eye manufacturer".

As the nineteenth century progressed, Directories were needed less for commercial purposes than to provide exact information of names and addresses for the benefit of the Post Office, to ensure the correct delivery of letters. Some of these Directories were published by the Post Office itself, many others by the firm of Kelly, who still produce them today. There is generally much less introductory information on towns and villages than in the earlier volumes, and it may prove at times not very accurate; but the information about the inhabitants is much fuller, each household, not just the more prosperous ones, being included. The more modern ones give details about the occupations of at least some of the people included, and about the general size of farms. With the aid of these Directories the history of your town or village can be taken up to the beginning of the Second World War, and in the case of towns, to even more recent times.

But just exactly how can the best use be made of these Directories? First you must make a list of those known for your area, and for this task you will need the help of your local librarian. The final count will probably amount to some fifteen or twenty for the period 1860 to 1940. Then you must get clear in your mind the questions you are going to ask. I have suggested that the introductions to each village or town, especially in the early Directories, will be of value, and these should be combed for information. Collect the information under separate headings, such as "Schools", "Transport" (coaches, railways, buses, carriers), "Town Government", "Industry", or any other topic you may find of interest. Then you will come to the names and occupations. Take the trades first, listing the numbers of different types in one year, and then comparing the numbers against those found in the next Directory. In this way you will be able to trace how some trades died out and others took their place. In most villages in the middle of the nineteenth century you would find at least one butcher, one grocer, one shoemaker and one carpenter. These have now, except in the larger villages, disappeared. By looking through each surviving Directory in turn you will be able to find out when these changes occurred. If you are dealing with a town you may notice that some traders were to be found in particular streets and not in others; this was common practice in earlier times, when butchers for example, who slaughtered animals on the premises, were discouraged from having their shops in the best parts of the town. Even in the nineteenth century, and in some places later, this kind of practice was common, and this, too, can be traced through the Directory by noting where each tradesman lived. There will be some streets of course, which were, at least in the early directories, purely residential; it is a valuable exercise to follow the history of some of these, showing how shops were gradually introduced. This information can then be usefully supplemented by information from Rate Books, which are dealt with later.

Apart from studies of streets and crafts, you can use Directories to trace particular institutions and buildings. They will give you a good start if you want to write the history of schools in your area, which you should then supplement by using the records of the schools themselves. They are very useful, too, for tracing the histories of mills, especially in villages, where it is often very difficult to find exactly when a mill ceased production. The Directory may help, too, if you want to begin to trace a family in a village or town.

These are only a selection of uses for local Directories; when you begin to use them, no doubt other questions will cross your mind, other uses will be found. One final suggestion: these books relied for financial support on local tradesmen who advertised in a special section, usually at the back, complete with a special index. These advertisements are often very interesting and amusing, such as the firm in Warwick which made among other things, corrugated iron buildings and road cleansing equipment. Their advertisement included a picture of one of their buildings— a church set amid palm trees—and a group of road machines including a dust cart which had won them a medal awarded by London County Council.

Newspapers
Most medium and large towns had one or more newspapers for at least part of the nineteenth century, and county newspapers usually give some information on even the smallest towns and villages. Such papers are not always easy to find, but your local librarian should be able to help you locate them. They are, of course, rather bulky, often being bound in volumes covering a year at a time, and the disappointing thing is that very few are indexed. This means that to search them properly would take a very long time, as well as being often rather boring and bad for your eyes. When you have looked at one or two issues you will notice that, unlike in our newspapers today, there is very little national or international news, except perhaps when there is an election or a war; that local news too is limited, though usually

to be found in the same place in each issue; and that the first
page and much space elsewhere is devoted to advertisements,
notices of sales, amusements, excursions and many other things.
It is very easy to get sidetracked into looking at these instead of
searching for one's own subject.

Early newspapers are often very biased in the way news is
reported, particularly at election time, or when the business of a
local council is concerned. As our national newspapers today
often reflect the opinion of the major political parties, so local
newspapers in the eighteenth and nineteenth centuries reflected
the views, often very extreme, of their proprietors. So before
placing much reliance on the news reported by your particular
paper, it will be wise to find out the political opinions of the
proprietor at the time. The many advertisements are not likely to
suffer so much in this way, and they will often prove to be the
most rewarding part of the newspaper for the general historian
of a town. There can be found, among other things, notices of
public meetings (which can often be followed up in the news
items of later issues), of sales of houses and land in and around
the town, of sports and plays, tradesmen's sales, notices of private
schools, and situations vacant.

To look at every surviving newspaper for your town would be
too large a task, and would not repay the work involved; to cover
even one year, you will find, will take some time. So before you
begin your search proper it will be a good idea to limit your study
to just one or two years, and then for a group to set to work,
each member looking for specific items. It is important to know
exactly what you are looking for. One, for example, will look for
news of a local election, another for anything about the town
council, another for material about schools, another for the local
theatre and other amusements such as balls and circuses, and so
on. Then choose another single year, fifteen or twenty years later,
and look for the same kind of things. If time permits you can make
a survey of this kind over a hundred years or more, provided your
local newspapers survive. You can then begin to compare the
findings, and see how the town council developed, how industry
grew or declined, how education increased, and how a town
cricket or football team began, perhaps even attaining wider fame
in a national division. One paper may be interesting, too many
can be boring; but if you select a few topics and search for them
in an organised way you will find newspapers of the greatest value.

Rate Books

A third general source for both villages and towns during the nineteenth century, and occasionally earlier, is the rate book. These, of course, may be found for earlier periods, but in great numbers from 1800 onwards. Though not always compiled by the same method, these give the names, and sometimes the addresses of every individual who was required to pay a small sum of money each year to the overseers of the poor, to the church-wardens, to surveyors of highways, and finally, as we still do, to local councils. Because of the different people to whom the money was paid, the books themselves may be found in several places. Overseers, churchwardens and highway surveyors usually left their records in the parish chest; they may still be there, or may now be in a local County Record Office. In a town, however, at least some of the overseers' records may have come into the custody of the town council, together with the town's own rate books.

Rate books, therefore, provide a list of at least the more substantial inhabitants of a town or village and, in the case of more modern ones, of all but the poorest. Sometimes the names of the payers are arranged alphabetically, with no indication of where they lived; at other times they are arranged by streets, though since houses were not usually numbered it will still not be possible to say exactly where a particular person lived unless you know how the list was compiled. If you know, for example, that the list for the main street of your town always begins with the same house, going down one side of the street and then back up the other, you will be able to look at rate books for each year in turn and trace the inhabitants of each house for as long as rate books survive. If, on the other hand, the order of compilation differs from year to year, you will not be able to do this.

Now this does not look very promising; what *can* be done with rate books? As I have mentioned above, if you are sure that the order of compilation is the same for each year, you can trace the occupants of, and perhaps identify, each house. From your Directories you may be able to find more about some of these occupants, including what trade they followed. If the house was a shop or a school, you may find more about it from local newspapers, or from the records of the town council or the parish records. From studying one house, you can go on to study a whole street in this way, showing whether it was residential or commercial in character, and whether, over the years, it changed from one to the other.

The rate books are also very valuable if you are studying a growing town. During the nineteenth century manufacturing towns grew very rapidly. Maps will show you in a general way how this came about but rate books will be able to date the changes more closely for, when new houses were built, the town council was not slow in demanding rates from them. Similarly, many towns had tenement houses wedged in behind the main streets, approached by narrow passages. These were on the whole inhabited by the very poor, but they may still figure in the rate books even if the occupants were too poor to pay. Unlike the streets of the nineteenth century, these have nearly all been demolished, and do not always show up on maps. With this information you will be able to draw plans of your town at various stages of its growth.

You will also want to go and look at these "new" streets for yourself. A street called Station Road or Railway Street will probably be in your list. The name will give you a clue as to how it came to be built—to join the old part of the town to the newly constructed railway station. It would probably have been built in the period 1850–80, and if you go there and look carefully at the buildings, you may find a date, probably on one of the gables, which confirms this estimate. Now you might try a "biography" of the street, to find out whether it was at first residential, or whether shops were built almost immediately to attract travellers as they passed to and from the railway. From there, still using Directories, you can follow any changes in the type of shop there, bringing the story up to date with a survey of your own. All kinds of questions may then crop up, such as whether or not any shops or firms were there in the 1880s and are still there now, and which is the oldest business in the street.

Railway Street leading to the railway brings us to another source for the history of towns, street and road names. Some of these names will, of course, be comparatively modern, but even these have their value. The streets and roads on modern housing estates are sometimes named after some famous local figure or event, sometimes after the old name for the fields on which the houses are built. In the older parts of towns, names may well recall something much earlier. Cheap Street, Cheapside, or Chipping nearly always indicate the site where the market stalls were set up in the Middle Ages. Many towns have a Victoria Street, named after the Queen, of course, and a Coronation Street, though which coronation this commemorates is not always easy to say; other towns will have a Canon Street, a Priory Row, a Chapel Street, or a Castle Hill, though very often no priory, chapel or castle is to be seen. The name at least serves as a clue. With the aid of Directories and rate books you may well be able to identify people after whom the streets were named in the nineteenth century and later. In Warwick, for example, you will find Crompton Street, Woodhouse Street and Parkes Street. The rate books show that they were first inhabited in the 1820s, and the Directories make clear that they were named after three of the town's leading industrialists, whose workers were housed there, and who no doubt were, therefore, responsible for building the streets. But not all names have such origins. Quite near these streets in Warwick is another, called Wallace Street. It was not named after a Mr. Wallace, but after a lion of the same name exhibited by a travelling showman, that fought with local bull-dogs, two at a time.

Directories, newspapers and rate books, if properly used, will enable you to write a very comprehensive history of your town and village at least from the middle of the nineteenth century until the present day.

Study suggestions

(a) Collect information under separate headings—such as schools, mills, transport, industry etc.—from each Directory for your town or village, and from your selection of local newspapers. Add any information you may find from rate books, and then piece your findings together.

(b) List the trades and occupations of your town or village from each Directory and show any changes. How have these come about?

(c) Information gathered under (a) above may be supplemented, for example by studying the records of your borough council, or the Log Books of a school.

(d) Write a "biography" of a house, finding all you can about the people who appear in the rate books as having lived in it.

(e) Write a "biography" of a street, showing any changes in its character. Try and account for these changes.

(f) Construct a diagrammatic map showing the growth of your town.

(g) Make a list of the streets in your neighbourhood. How did their names originate?

Where are the Sources?

Directories: Ask your local librarian. He may have a complete set, or he may know where particular volumes are to be found.

Newspapers: Again ask your librarian. Complete sets of old newspapers are rare.

Rate Books: Parish rate books are usually kept in the "parish chest", though many parishes have now deposited their records at County Record Offices. Check first with the County Archivist. Rate books for towns are more likely to be found in the custody of the Town Clerk.

Council Minutes: Again, the originals are most likely to be at the Town Hall, though printed copies may be held at the borough library. Check first with the librarian.

VIII

Recording Memories

THROUGHOUT this book we have been dealing very largely with written sources of history, with books and manuscripts in which people have recorded information for their own or somebody else's use. And in order to write the history of our own town or village we, too, will have written down some parts of these books and papers; and we may well have traced parts of maps and even sketched or photographed buildings or roads or streams. Through all these methods, we will have recorded what we want of things we can *see*. But you will find as you begin to study the more recent past that you have to use another kind of source, people's memories; and the best way to make use of them is not to write down what they say but to record it on tape. The memories of people who have lived in a town or village all their lives will tell you more about the life of the people of the place than you can possibly find in books. But you must always bear in mind when you are asking people questions, whether for recording or not, that the answers may not be as accurate as you would like.

Just to demonstrate this, try to remember what the weather was like a week ago, or when you first sailed in a boat, or the day you were last ill in bed. And then remember that you are asking people to recall events as much as fifty years ago. You will sometimes be surprised how old people, in particular, can remember very small details of what happened in their childhood, but cannot so easily think of events of much more recent date.

This difficulty is not a new one. In the Middle Ages, if property was inherited by a child, it was held by a guardian until the heir came of age. But before he or she could have the property, there had to be proof that the heir was of the right age. This was before the days of birth certificates; the only way to do it was to find enough people who remembered when the heir was born or

75

baptised. And when they came to give evidence they usually had to say exactly how they remembered the event. Many of them had been invited to the christening in order that they might give such evidence if required. Others were neighbours who remembered because they had a child born at the same time, or because they recalled seeing the name of the newly-christened child written in the mass book of the parish church. Still others remembered because of something which had happened to them at the time, such as losses of cattle through disease, or some personal accident: for example, a man might have fallen from his horse and broken his leg after the christening!

Now the same sort of answers are often given today. If you ask when a house was pulled down, a chapel closed, or a farm sold, you often will be told "when my mother was still alive", or "when I was a little girl". To demonstrate this to yourselves, get two old people to talk about something you know for certain from another source and compare the answers!

But the memories of old people are extremely valuable for gathering impressions of life, if not actual facts. Get your grandparents to talk about their schooldays, and you will find material to supplement what is to be found in the school log book. They will remember what the teachers were like, what lessons they learnt, and what they did at play. And once you get them talking about the past you will hear how things have changed; they will talk about going to work, about wages and prices, about factories and working conditions there, or about farms and the many labourers employed on them. I have heard people talking about the shepherds, carters and ploughboys, about women hoeing turnips or making butter and cheese. Only a few weeks ago I discovered that my own grandmother when a girl had lived in an old farmhouse in which I was interested. Her father was not the owner, but leased the dairy—that is, rented the farmer's cows and pasture, and sold the produce. These were days before the First World War, before milk was sold to factories, processed, bottled, and taken to towns for sale. It was all turned into butter in the dairy, and my grandmother remembers making over a hundred pounds of butter before breakfast each morning, and as much after breakfast. Then she talked of their neighbours of those days, and of how they fell out with the vicar. She could even remember the vicar's name and I, who had found his name elsewhere, could prompt her to recall other things about him.

Another old lady, in a Wiltshire village, loved to talk of her schooldays. A canal ran through the southern tip of the parish. With the coming of the railways most of these canals lost their trade, so it was a very exciting occasion when news came that a barge was on its way. She and her friends would rush out of school to see it as it glided along. Many people, of course, will be able to tell you about the early days of motor cars, of electricity, of radio, things which we now take so much for granted.

These and many other topics need to be recorded, to be taken down not only for our own use, but for others also. How are we to go about this? How best can we preserve these memories?

Tape Recorders

A first step is to get these memories down on tape. Some people become shy when you put a microphone in front of them, so get them talking first! You are sure to get long pauses, "ums" and "ers", much repetition, information which you will later find of no use at all; but from perhaps a dozen interviews of this kind you will be able to build up a picture of life in your town or village fifty years ago. You will have to cut and edit, often a good deal, but gradually something will emerge. You need a balanced picture, so be sure that as well as interviewing farm workers or factory employees you talk to farmers and factory owners, if you can find them. And, incidentally, don't think of factories as huge places where hundreds of people work. I was talking only two weeks ago to a man whose father made the first car in Taunton, in about 1906. The Taunton Chassis Construction Company made just one car, but it would, I suppose, count as a factory. Choose your "victims" to give you some idea of general life in the past, as well as particular branches of activity: so, to give you some idea of prices of food and clothes, talk to house-wives; of changes in education, find retired teachers as well as pupils!

Some people will talk without much prompting. When you have conducted a number of interviews, listen to them and try to see what gaps you have. Then talk to those who might be more shy of the microphone. People will generally talk about their early years, however shy they are, but they may have to be prompted to describe their homes and the streets where they lived, to re-member the rare trips to London or the visit of some circus or fair, now long since forgotten. Sometimes you will find you have to produce some forgotten memory given you by someone else to jog another memory, or show someone an old photograph. Such things very often produce so many new facts that without a tape recorder you would be quite overwhelmed.

Using the material

Before you start editing proper, you will have to decide how you are going to present your material. There are a number of methods you can use. There is, however, one point of importance: you must always make sure to record the name and age of the person talking. So very often people will say "When I was a boy . . ." and if you don't know roughly when they were born you, and therefore your readers and listeners, won't know what years are being talked about.

There are, of course, a number of different ways you can use the material you have collected on tape, and the following few are by no means the only ones:

(a) To supplement written material by including facts from tapes in your own written history. So for example, in writing the history of a school, you include information taken from the memories of some of the first pupils, about, say, the lessons or the teachers. This may also be done by writing complete extracts (if not too long) from the tapes about this one topic. After your own notes on the school, therefore, you may write: "Mrs. Cornworthy of Sutton, now aged 87, attended the school between 1888 and 1896. She remembers 'Miss Allen, the headmistress, a very strict woman . . . etc., etc. etc.'."

(b) Another use of tapes is to compile a "programme", with music or commentary, on particular subjects, such as "Farm Work in the 1920s" or "Early Motor Cars", or some other subject of your choice. These tapes may be the results of your asking questions on these very subjects, or they may have to be edited from much longer tapes. That depends on you.

(c) The tapes may also be used as "commentaries" for slides or other photographs or pictures. If you show an old photograph to an old person, the result is often a stream of comment about it —maybe an old building, or a Sunday School outing or a street scene. So why not show the same photographs to your audience at school, and play back the tape for their benefit?

Editing tapes needs to be carefully and skillfully done, but you will find it very worthwhile. Just to listen to people with long memories brings the past back to life, and provides the link between the many documents with which this book has been concerned and the things we can still see in our towns and villages.

PART TWO

I

The Parish of Wilton, Somerset

YOU will remember that in the Introduction to this book there was a discussion about choosing which parish to study; and the conclusion was that if there was enough suitable material, one's own parish would often be the best choice. This is certainly true in my case. There is ample material for the kind of study I have been suggesting, and in the following pages will be found some of those topics which have been dealt with in this book. They have been arranged to coincide with the chapter headings, but information from one source can often be used to help in several topics, so you will find maps, for example, being used in various places.

We began with maps. The oldest one for Wilton alone is rather a rare type. It is kept in the church safe still, and was drawn for the parish, to be included in a *Survey of the Parish of Wilton, 1821.* Two parts of this map are illustrated in plates 3 and 4. The map itself measures more than three feet wide by more than one foot high, and shows, in colour, all the houses and gardens as well as fields (whether arable or pasture), roads and hedges. Each property is numbered, and the rest of the survey lists all the owners and tenants, the value of the land, and the amount of rates they had to pay to the churchwardens for the upkeep of the church. It was the basis of the parish rate until 1878.

The next map to be made of Wilton parish was the tithe map of 1840, kept with the tithe award in the County Record Office. This map is not coloured, but shows similar detail to the older one, each piece of land being numbered and described, and its ownership listed. Two other maps I have used a great deal are the first edition of the 6″ Ordnance Survey map, made in 1886 and published in 1889 (sheet LXX SE), a copy of which is in the County Record

Office, and the modern 2½″ Ordnance Survey map (sheet ST 22).

This last map shows, at a glance, where Wilton lies, on the southern and south-western boundaries of Taunton, the county town of Somerset. It is a good plan to begin your history with a description of the position of your parish in relation especially to its nearest town, and then to describe its physical features, its boundaries, roads and waterways.

Wilton is so near Taunton that much of the parish is now within

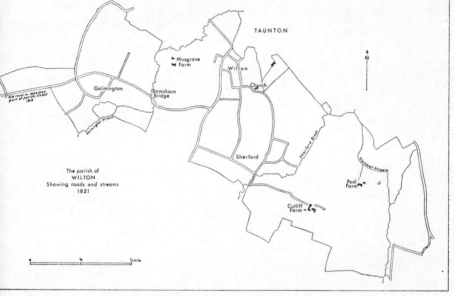

Fig. IV. The Parish of Wilton, 1821

the municipal borough. For much longer it has been a suburb where prosperous men have built large houses surrounded by their own grounds in preference to living in the centre of the town over their shops. It has, too, provided space for a specu-lator to build small houses for workers in the town. These facts have had an important effect on the character of the parish and its buildings (see p. 88). In more recent times, and particularly since the Second World War, the expansion of population in Taunton has meant that more and more land in the parish has been developed for housing, so that what was once partly "country" and partly "residential" has become "suburban".

Like Taunton, Wilton is low-lying, reaching little more than 150 feet above sea level at its highest point. The parish is, in fact, divided by a ridge, followed by the Trull road, the land falling away from it to Galmington on the west and to Wilton and Sherford on the east.

The boundaries of the parish as found in the maps of 1821 and 1840 differ from those on the more modern maps. The former are the "ancient" ones of the ecclesiastical parish, enclosing those

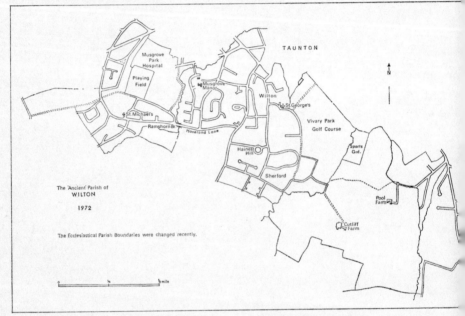

FIG. V. The "Ancient" Parish of Wilton, 1972

lands whose owners or occupiers paid tithe to the church. How "ancient" we shall never know. The modern boundaries are of the "civil" parish, an area delimited for reasons of local government administration. The "ancient" boundaries are those which should be the starting point for the local historian.

There is no Saxon charter for Wilton describing the boundaries, for Wilton was but one of many settlements within the great manor of Taunton belonging to the Bishop of Winchester. We shall have to describe the parish by looking only at the 1821 map. And it is noticeable that the line very often follows a natural feature—a stream, or an ancient road. The "ancient" parish, not counting small fields some distance away from the main parish, was about 2¼ miles from east to west, and a mile at the most from north to south. The boundaries are, as can be seen, very irregular, simply because natural features were followed. The sketch map in Figure IV shows also the roads as they existed in 1821. Compare these with Figure V, where modern roads serving new housing areas are included. From the lines of roads alone, it is possible to see very clearly how the parish has changed in the last twenty years; how the residential area of Taunton has spread into this ancient country parish, leaving only one farm where there had once been nearly as many farms as houses.

Now let us turn to the more modern maps. A few yards south-east of the church, in Cherry-Tree Lane, is a spot marked as the site where, in 1879, a small hoard of bronze implements of the middle or third quarter of the Bronze Age was found. These, however, are not the earliest archaeological remains, for in 1853, according to the *Proceedings of the Somerset Archaeological Society* (volume lxxxviii, p. 16), some deep excavations at the northern end of the parish "revealed a prehistoric forest of oak, alder, willow and hazel, with acorns and hazel-nuts, embedded in leaf-mould. Parts of eleven immense oak trees, excellently preserved, were discovered; one was 60 feet long. These trees may have flourished in the Neolithic or early Bronze Age (about 2500–1800 B.C.), and have been killed by subsidence of the land causing the river or the tributaries to overflow and deposit the clay beds. The skull and a few bones of a Woolly Rhinoceros were recovered from the same site, but at a higher level, at a depth of only 6 feet. The animal lived in the glacial period, and the remains were perhaps washed down with clay from the neighbouring hills."

These finds, and particularly the bronze implements, serve to remind us to ask the question "How old is Wilton?" This is a question which cannot be precisely answered. It used to be thought that a Roman road ran through the parish (see fig. IV) crossing a stream by Ramshorn Bridge (plate 5), and this was still claimed by the surveyors who drew the first edition of the 6″ Ordnance Survey map in 1886. There is not a scrap of evidence for this belief. But the "-ton" part of the name Wilton is a word of Saxon origin meaning settlement, and we know that a church of stone stood there in Saxon times, parts of which still survive in the west wall of the present parish church.

The "-ton" means a Saxon settlement; the "Wil-" probably

L.S.—4

explains why this particular spot was chosen, for an early form of the name is spelt "Weltoune", Well-town. There was, it seems, a well or spring here. To ancient people water had sacred qualities: the owners of the Bronze implements may perhaps have worshipped some god at that spring, and a Saxon Christian missionary may have put that fact to good use by dedicating this sacred spot to the worship of God by building a small church there. The well, of course, remained, and was later, like the church, dedicated to St. George. *Fons Sancti Georgii*, the Latin name for the area, meaning the Well of St. George, is still remembered in the parish as the name of a road near the church, called Fons George.

With the aid of maps we have made a start with the history of the parish, tracing the possible origins of the settlement at Wilton. There are, as can be seen from the maps in plates 3 and 4, two other hamlets in the parish, Galmington (often called Gaunton earlier), and Sherford. The first, with a "-ton" ending, is an indication of another Saxon settlement. In 1821 it was very small, the largest house being that now called "Manor House". Sherford, the other hamlet, is, as its name suggests, near a stream, the Sherford Brook. This name is also Saxon in origin.

Now what can the field names teach us? Wilton lies in that part of Somerset which was *not* cultivated in: large tracts of arable fields divided into tiny strips. Its fields have long been enclosed in some fashion, though this is not to say that changes have not taken place (for some changes on one farm see figs. VI and VII). The field names will not, therefore, enable us to reconstruct one of these large fields, and the parish had no park for deer. They do not give a great deal of help at all. Many have names describing their area, such as "the Five Acres", "Yonder Seven Acres", "Three Acres at Gaunton Water"; or by their cultivation, like "Gaunton Ash Orchard", "Wilton Meadow". Some, like "Shoulder of Mutton Field", are so called by their shape; others by the name of an owner or former owner, like "Can's Field" or "Haines's Five Acres" (see p. 104); still others because of a building in it, as "Linhay Field", a linhay being an open-sided shed for cattle or implements. And there are problem names, the reasons for which are not known, such as "Clapping Gates", "The Raps", or "Brick Meadow" (though a man called William Pursey, brickmaker, occurs in the parish register from 1813–24).

Boundaries, roads, fields. Now what of rivers and streams? The sketch maps (figs. IV and V) show three streams in the

parish: one of these, the brook of Syreford or Sherford, is mentioned as early as 1129, or perhaps earlier. William Giffard,
bishop of Winchester 1107–29, gave the manor of Fons George
to Taunton Priory, and with it the course of this brook "for
grinding their corn and all advantage thence to be derived". The
mill for the corn lay just outside the parish, in Taunton itself, but
the stream also fed the priory's fish ponds, now of course disappeared but remembered in the name Vivary Park, after *vivarium*,
the Latin name for a fish pond.

Boundaries, roads, field-names and streams have given us the
beginnings of the history of Wilton. They will tell us much about
almost every town and village. In this Wilton is typical. But it is
not typical, in that it is a suburb of a town; this fact adds much
to its interest. And one other feature makes Wilton special. A
careful look at Wilton in 1821 (plate 3) will reveal a large building
numbered 14 and marked "Gaol". This was the gaol for the
county established about 1755. The building still stands today,
though not now used as a gaol.

On the whole it affected the life of the parish very little, though
if you look at the census figures for, say, 1831 you will find that although the total population of the parish was 795, 113 were prisoners in the gaol, and only 682 lived in Wilton by choice. Most
references to the gaol in our sources are found in the parish registers:

Baptisms: 9 Nov. 1813: Jane, Eliza and Frederick, children of
Alexander Gane, gaoler, and Rachel his
wife.

6 Nov. 1824: Moses Jackson, prisoner.

23 Nov. 1824: Charles, son of Mary Fudge, and
Elizabeth, daughter of Mary Brice, both
prisoners.

12 Oct. 1834: Henry, son of Long John, turnkey at
Wilton gaol, and Mary his wife.

And among the Burials:

14 Jan. 1818: Adam Owen of Wilton gaol, aged 74.

17 Mar. 1821: Charles Martin of Wilton gaol, aged 23.

24 Nov. 1824: William Farrant of Wilton gaol, aged 82.

13 Apr. 1825: Ann Pain of Wilton House of Correction,
aged 3 months.

2 June 1825: John Hole of Wilton House of Correction,
aged 12 weeks.

14 Apr. 1827: John Townsend of Wilton House of
Correction, aged 73.

The People of the Parish

The parish of Wilton lay, as we have seen, within the Bishop of Winchester's great manor of Taunton, and was therefore neither mentioned by name nor described separately in *Domesday Book*. We know the place existed then because, as we have also seen, there is Saxon masonry in part of the parish church, and the names Wilton, Sherford and Galmington are Saxon in origin.

So we can learn little of the people of the parish until 1327. In that year a tax was raised, and the names of all those who had to pay it were recorded on a subsidy roll, which has been printed by the *Somerset Record Society*. The roll shows us that the parish was then divided into two parts, because the Bishop of Winchester had given part of his estate there to the prior of Taunton (see p. 85). This part of the parish was then called Fons Prioris, the prior's spring or well. The remainder of the parish, still held by the bishop, was called Galmetone cum Shireforde (Galmington with Sherford). These two hamlets were then the richest parts of the parish, raising 16/4d. between them, compared with the 3/5d. of Fons Prioris. Richard atte Brigge was the wealthiest man there, and had to pay 4/–; his name must come from one of the bridges crossing the stream either at Sherford or Galmington. He was followed in wealth by Margery Kynel who paid 3/–, Thomas Wille who paid 2/9d. and Thomas de Mousegreue who paid 2/6d. This last man took his name from that part of Galmington still called Musgrove. After these people came Nicholas Dawe (1/6d.), Adam Ricard, Richard Coppe, and Matilda Pare (each 8d.), and Richard Hernogz (7d.).

Only five people, all men, paid the tax in Fons Prioris: Adam Kemp (1/–), Thomas le Kyng (10d.), Richard Boketor (7d.), and Thomas atte Wille (? at the Well), and Richard Elisaundre (Alexander) (each 6d.).

So altogether we know the names of fourteen people of the parish in 1327, four of whom were called Richard. From their names we cannot guess what they did for a living, though one possibly lived near a bridge, another near a well. Almost certainly most of them were farmers.

The lists of payers of the Poll Tax in Wilton, as in most places in Somerset, has not survived, and no more subsidy rolls have yet been printed. But we can learn just a little more about some men of the parish from a complaint John de Hembury of Taunton made to King Edward III in 1338 and preserved in a letter the

king sent to his judges asking them to deal with the matter
(*Calendar of Patent Rolls* 1338–1340, p. 65). It appears that two
brothers, Thomas and John de Orchard, with others, had broken
down a hedge around one of John de Hembury's fields in
"Weltoune", and had taken away 6 oxen, worth £6 13s. 4d.

The people of Wilton parish have left a few wills for us to study,
and at least one of these has been printed. It was drawn up by
Simon Fyschare, or Fisher, in 1505. He was, as he says, a merchant
from Taunton, and was clearly very prosperous. One of his
possessions was a farm at Wilton called Osbrondesal Place, which
he held from the prior of Taunton, and which he passed on to his
son, Alexander. Still today the names Osborne Place and Osborne
Grove can be found in the parish to remind us of this farm.

Before we move to the Hearth Tax lists of the seventeenth
century, here are extracts from two other sources, not mentioned
earlier in the book because in most cases they may well be difficult
to read. Almost certainly they will not be printed, but these
particular ones were found in the County Record Office, and your
archivist may be able to point out similar stories for the parish
of your choice. The first comes from the records of the court of
the Bishop of Bath and Wells. The writing is not easy to read and
many of the words are in Latin. Most of this particular incident is
told in English, and concerns James Jones, curate of Wilton. He
found himself in court in 1606

for marryeing diverse persons at unlawfull tymes and namelie uppon
the xixth of Julye last about noone he married a couple being strangers
(whooe present thearat theie knowe not). And on the morrowe
following being Sondaie about xij a clock at midnight he did solennize
another mariage in theire churche betweene a stranger being a man
of Mr. Courtnies in Devon and a maide of Mr. Waldrons at Sea as
it is reported. Whooe present they knowe not but one Joane Jordan
and the wydowe Addams two poor woomen whooe looked in at the
windowes of the church and saw the same and gave notice therof
unto the wardens. . . .

Some of the people at Wilton were evidently very curious, and
others quarrelled among themselves. The following extracts come
from the records of the court of Quarter Session, also found at
the County Record Office, and refer to the year 1690. Exactly
what the trouble was about, we do not know, but George Clement,
a worker in worsted cloth, and Philip Slocombe of Galmington,

were enemies. George told the magistrates that he had heard
Philip say that a third man, John Warren, also of Galmington, was
a "stealing rogue, grasse stealing rogue and pick lock". Philip in
his turn reported George to the magistrates, but before his complaint was heard, George also complained, and Philip was taken
off to gaol and roughly handled. On the way he was "violently
abused", and dragged along the ground,

> which occasioned this informant earnestly to request them (the
> constables) not to offer him such violence, telling them that one of
> his ribs had been almost broken already. The Guard replied "God
> rott thee, I'll break two or three more of thy ribs before we parte".
> They put him on a horse to take him to the gaol and "girted him with
> a pack girt with his head backwards and his feet forwards upon the
> horse'. Once they stopped at an Inn, but when he wanted to lie down
> he was pulled off the bed and the guard "swore he would pull his
> flesh off his bones and make him go home bare boned".

Hearth Tax returns survive for Wilton for 1664 and 1665.
Seventeen houses were there mentioned, though probably the
largest was included by mistake. The largest certainly in Wilton
was that of George Browne with 7 hearths, followed by those of
George Powell, George Lissant and Nathaniel Quash with 6 each.
Mr. Quash's house was in the possession of "very poor tenants",
and they were therefore not forced to pay. Widow Cade's house
had 5 hearths, William Durston's 4, three houses had 3 hearths,
five had 2, and two had only 1. We will deal with these houses
again in the next section, but these figures show us something
important about Wilton which later was to become characteristic;
that it attracted prosperous people. A house with more than two
or three hearths is probably that of a well-to-do man, and 9 out of
16 houses in Wilton had 3 or more. And one man for certain,
George Browne, was a professional man with a business in
Taunton who preferred to live some distance from his office.
Mr. Browne was Clerk of the Castle for the Bishop of Winchester,
the agent for the bishop's large estate around Taunton.

And how did the people of the parish live? Their houses will
come later, but we can see by looking at the inventories of their
goods how different they were. All had beds and tables, sheets
and spoons, pots and pans, but some had things which only a
prosperous man would buy, because he liked them, or because he
liked to be in fashion. So let us end this section with extracts

from the inventories of George Browne (died 1679), George Powell (died 1684), and Ames Blinman (died 1688):

George Browne

> Bookes   £10
> Silver plate   £6
> In the parlour: Item one tableboard, one sideboard and halfe dozen of chaires, halfe dozen of high stooles and two low stooles two carpetts one paire of Brasse Andirons one paire of Fire Dogs with Brasse topps two Violls one Landskip two Face Pictures and one Iron back   £8
> ... Item one Birding piece   12s.
> ... Item Four pair of Holland sheetes   £3 10s.
> ... For things forgotten and out of sight   £1   6s.
>
>   ... total   £211 8s.

So Mr. Browne liked books, probably law books, since he was dealing with legal matters for the Bishop of Winchester; he liked music (or perhaps his family did), for he played the viol, the ancestor of the violin; he had some pictures—a landscape and two portraits; a gun for shooting birds, sheets of the best quality. A prosperous man.

George Powell (his inventory was destroyed in the war, and only notes on it survive)

> Plate, weighing 373 ozs. 18 dwt.   £93 9s. 6d.
> Four Spanish tables
> Small hower glasses
>   ... total   £779 3s. 9d.

Ames Blinman   In 1664–5, according to the Hearth Tax returns, he was living in a house with only one hearth. In view of his obvious prosperity by the time of his death in 1688, he had either moved, or built his old house into the latest fashion. His inventory mentions eleven rooms as well as outhouses and barns. When he died he had a vast number of possessions including:

> Two birding pieces in the hall
> A "pair of harpsichards and frame" in the parlour
> A clock on the staircase
> A sword and a case of pistols in a barn
> Two "chamber potts" worth 2s. in the timber chamber

Mr. Blinman, according to the parish register, was buried on March 25, 1688, and from the same register we can construct a part of his family tree: Ames Blinman (d. 1688) married (in 1655) Dorothy Durston (d. 1669).

Mr. Blinman died a very wealthy man, at least in theory. His goods were valued at nearly £500, but over £392 was owed to him, described as "money due to the deceased on bonds or otherwise".

These are just some of the people of the parish.

Houses and farms

From the Hearth Tax Returns of 1664–5 we have seen that Wilton parish contained a number of substantial houses, many of them farmhouses, but one or two the residences of Taunton businessmen. At least four, and probably more, are still standing, though it is difficult if not impossible to say which was which without tracing the history of each house back from the present day. And all of them have, of course, been very much altered. Widow Cade's house in 1665 had only five hearths, but the present house at Musgrove, the descendant of Widow Cade's home, is now divided into two dwellings and has more: it has clearly been very much altered if not completely rebuilt. Another house in the parish, Sherford House, was built after the Hearth Tax Return was made, for it has a moulded plaster overmantel with the date 1679. The "Manor House" at Galmington (plate 8), one of the oldest houses in the parish, must be included somewhere in the Return, but at the moment it is not possible to find who owned it at the time. So, apart from being able to say how many hearths the larger houses in the parish had at the time, we are no further forward.

But as it happens a number of inventories have survived for the period 1679–88 which give us glimpses into several houses in the parish. There is, for example, the inventory of Thomas Evans (1680). He was a small farmer, and possibly also an innkeeper. He had two oxen, three heifers and a calf, 23 sheep and four lambs, a horse and two pigs. There were a few farm implements and a quantity of peas and barley in his barn; but he does not seem to have had a farmyard, for his two hayricks (spelt "haireeks") were standing on other farms. Also in his possession when he died were 13 large barrels of cider, known as hogsheads, worth £1 each, 26 empty hogsheads, 10 tubs, 6 barrels and a "trendle". If he was an innkeeper, what kind of house did he have?

The rooms mentioned in the inventory are hall, kitchen, and

THE PARISH OF WILTON, SOMERSET

hall chamber; a very small house, with one room up, one down, and the kitchen probably built on at the rear. The hall was nearly bare, having a table, 6 stools, and a chest, very likely the place where his customers drank their cider. There is no mention of fire irons, and the room was therefore probably not heated. These implements were in the kitchen: the hooks for hanging pots over the fire, the spits on which joints of meat were roasted. Upstairs, in the hall chamber, were two bedsteads, two feather beds, two pairs of sheets and a few other things. Not the house of a rich man by any means, a house with only one hearth.

In contrast, there was George Browne, who paid tax on seven hearths in 1664–5. The inventory of Mr. Browne's goods made in 1679 shows a house with a large number of rooms, and the references to fire irons show exactly where the hearths were. In this house, on the ground floor, there was a hall, a parlour, a kitchen, a larder, a buttery, and a dairy. Fire irons are mentioned in the hall, the parlour, and, of course, the kitchen. In the latter there were evidently two hearths, for there were a pair of fire grates, a pair of spits, and as many as five pairs of pothooks. Upstairs there were rooms over the hall, parlour, kitchen, dairy and buttery, and a small room over the porch; and there were attics above the buttery and kitchen chambers. Fire irons are mentioned in the rooms over hall, buttery and kitchen. This makes a total of seven hearths, the number for which Mr. Browne paid in 1664–5.

One house standing in 1664–5 which can still be identified, is Cutliffe Farmhouse, in the seventeenth century the home of the Powell family. The inventory of the goods of George Powell, made in 1684, has only survived in note form, but it is possible to get some idea of the size of the house at the time:

Ground floor: Hall, great parlour, little parlour, kitchen;
First floor: Hall chamber, great parlour chamber, little parlour chamber, closet adjoining, study, chamber at head of stairs;
Attics: Upper, inner, and outer cockloft;
Outbuildings: pump court, dairy, bunting (chaff) house, little and long cellars.

The present house is largely built of brick, as far as can be seen from the outside, but there are indications that it was not built all at once. At the rear, for example, is a brick wing of two storeys which has been added. On the ground floor this has the remains

L.S.—4*

of a very beautiful room, with a moulded plaster ceiling and two very large windows, now bricked up. It seems likely that this wing was what in Mr. Powell's day was called the little parlour and little parlour chamber.

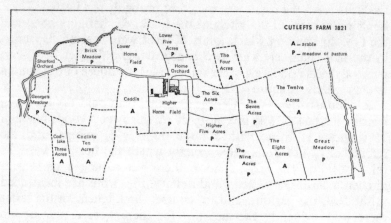

FIG. VI. Cutlefts Farm, 1821

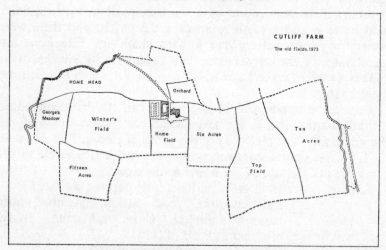

FIG. VII. Cutliffe Farm; the old fields, 1973

Of course the house has been very much altered even since that time: the present kitchen is what was once the great parlour and has a large fireplace and carved beams; the old kitchen, at the other end of the house, is not now used. It still has a fireplace, of course, one of the six mentioned in the Hearth Tax returns under

Mr. Powell's name; but without the inventory we cannot tell where all the others were.

Cutliffe Farm also illustrates how changes in farming can be seen through a careful study of farm buildings. In 1684 Mr. Powell's farm stock comprised 43 sheep, 3 cows, 2 heifers, 11 oxen and steers, and a "nagg". He had, therefore, a mixed farm, producing wool and corn, for the oxen would be used for ploughing. The cows would provide just enough milk for butter and cheese for the family and employees. On the map of 1821 (fig. VI) we can see the layout of the farm buildings at that time: a long narrow building with two wings facing the side of the farmhouse, and three smaller sheds. Parts of the large building still remain, including a brick stable and a stone cattle shed. By the end of the nineteenth century, as can be seen from the 6″ map of the area, these buildings had been converted into part of a rectangular group around a yard, probably including cowsheds and stock pens. Dairying had by this time become important, taking the place of sheep and arable farming, so sheds were needed for milking the cows and rearing calves. Today the farmer has added dutch barns, providing space to store hay and straw for his stock; some of the sheds are used to store potatoes, which he grows in some quantity, and the stables no longer house horses. Larger spaces are needed for tractors and other modern equipment.

The farm, like the house, has thus changed very greatly over the years. The names of its fields are often different, and it is now much larger than it was in 1821 or in Mr. Powell's time. But Mr. Powell's house and the farm buildings of 1821 can still be seen. This is the case with hundreds of farmhouses and farmyards throughout the country.

The Parish Church
The parish church of Wilton is dedicated to St. George, the saint who became popular at the end of the twelfth century, at the time of the Third Crusade. But we can tell from the way part of the west wall of the church is built that it is older than that. We can be quite certain that there was a small church on the same spot in Saxon times, well before the Norman Conquest. The church is still small, seating only about 220 people, but it was much smaller at the beginning, just a chapel belonging to Taunton Priory, built on the Priory's estate, Fons George.

How the building itself has changed is a matter for experts. You can see by looking at the west wall, each side of the tower, where the old Saxon work ends and the later work begins. This shows that the early building has at some time been made wider. The shape of the pillars and of the arches inside the church tell experts that the aisles were begun in the thirteenth century, that the arches between the pillars were altered in the fifteenth century, and that most of the windows were made probably in the sixteenth century. After that time little seems to have been done to alter the building until the nineteenth century. In 1837–8 some very extensive rebuilding was done under the direction of an architect who lived in the parish, Richard Carver (see p. 103). What Mr. Carver did can best be seen by comparing the two paintings of the church, made before and after the work was done (plates 10 and 11). At a later date, 1852, a new tower was built after his design, replacing the one seen in those two general pictures of the church, and more closely in plate 12.

The churchyard at Wilton does not have any very old tombstones, though there are one or two "table" tombs, including that of Sir Benjamin Hammet, and those of Richard Carver, the architect, and of Thomas Burton, who built Burton Place (see p. 102). Inside the church, on the south wall, is a large monument commemorating Sir Benjamin Hammet. He died in 1800, and you will find in the parish register that he was buried on August 5. Sir Benjamin was a very wealthy man, was Member of Parliament for Taunton, and gave his name to a street in the town (see p. 100).

On the same wall as this monument, above the door, is a very fine carved coat of arms of King George III. Below the arms on a scroll, with the motto, is the following:

17   R. Culverwell   87

Who was R. Culverwell? The answer ought to be in the accounts of the churchwardens, which begin at Wilton in 1712, but the accounts for 1787 and 1788 are, for some reason, missing. We may never know who he was or where he lived, or how much he charged for his work. But from the same accounts, under the year 1827, we find that the arms needed attention, and the "gilding and painting" cost £3 10s.

These accounts and other papers will be able to tell us a great deal about many of the things we see in the church—the pulpit, how much it cost and when it was made; the pews, and when they were fitted. There is little about the glass in the accounts, but careful examination will show that most of it was put in during the later years of the nineteenth century, often as a memorial to some parishioner. But one or two pieces of glass, at the top of a window in the north aisle, look quite different from the rest. A careful examination reveals two small coats of arms, one of which has beneath it the words:

   George Powell of D(   ) and of Wilton in Somerset

We have already met this George Powell, but why should glass in the north aisle bear his name? An entry in the parish register explains part of the reason:

> Memorandum that George Powell of Wilton Gent. in the year (*blank*) by an agreement with the then officers and parishioners of Wilton did buy the North Isle of the Church (for a pew and burying place to be repaired by the said George and his heirs) for the sum of Forty shillings, . . .

So Mr. Powell was evidently a prosperous man. Can anything more be found about him? From the parish registers we can discover the following entries:

1667   Hanna the wife of George Powell gentel^m was buried the 29 of October

1672   Amia Powell daughter of George Powell gentelman and Drothy his wife was baptized the second day of July by Emanual Sharp vicker of Taunton

1673   Amia Powell daughter of George Powell gentelman & Dorothy his wife was buried the seventh of February in the Vault at Wilton

1673   Dorothy Powell, daughter of George Powell gentelman and Dorothy his wife was baptized the third of November 1673 by Emunuel Sharp Vicker of Taunton

1674   The first begotten son of George Powell gentelman and Dorothy his wife was borne the 13th of January 1674 and chrisned by Mr. Ema. Sharp, George Wood, the 11th February 1674

1674   Dorothy Powell daughter of George Powell gentelman & Dorothy his wife was buried the sixteenth of December in the Vault at Wilton

1676   John the son of George Powell gent. and Dorothy his wife was born 21th Novem and was chrisned 23d. November following being the second sonne

1678   Roger the son of George Powell gent and Dorothy his wife was borne the 7th of Aprill and baptised the 15th May being the third sonne

1684   Mrs. Dorothy Powell wid(ow) was buried August the 29th 1684

There is no mention, as you see, about the death of George Powell, though since Mrs. Powell was a widow at her death, he must have died between 1678 (when his youngest son was born) and August 29, 1684.

Let us, for a moment, return to the aisle and the vault, the "burying place" which George Powell bought, and where his two small daughters Amia and Dorothy, and probably his wife, were buried. When the church was being rebuilt in 1837 workmen found this vault behind the pulpit, about where the present organ now stands, and inside they found a huge stone coffin, 7 feet 9 inches long, all ready to hold a normal wooden coffin, and bearing an inscription in Latin. This states that the body of George Powell was buried inside, and that he died in the (blank) day of the (blank) month in the (blank) year. In fact he was never buried there at all. He must have died while away from Wilton, which accounts not only for the empty coffin, but also for the fact that his name is not entered in the parish register. Exactly when he died we do not know, but a note of his will (the original was destroyed in Exeter during the War) shows that he died between May 5, 1683 and the end of August 1684.

We can now draw up a small family "tree" for the family:

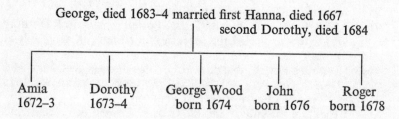

We have arrived at this genealogy of the Powell family by looking at the decorations and furnishings inside the church, and then at the parish registers. Let us now use the registers to study a poor, rather than a rich family; a family which could not afford even the luxury of a tombstone in the churchyard, let alone a monument inside, or a piece of stained glass window. This family lived in the poorest part of the parish, in Turkey Court.

From 1813 onwards the registers to be found in all churches conform to the same pattern: each page is arranged in columns, and much more information is given than in the earlier volumes. For this reason it is possible to study the occupations of the people of your parish before Directories appear, since this information is required to be written down in the register of baptisms. So looking down the column headed "Quality, Trade or Profession", the word "Fishmonger" is found, after the name of Richard Buston, who was living in Turkey Court in 1813 with his wife Mary and their little son, Charles, whom they brought to be baptised on March 14, in that year. Selling fish was a Buston family occupation: John and Ann Buston, also living in Turkey Court, were fishmongers, and their daughter, Jane, was baptised on February 27, 1814. In February 1816 Richard and Mary brought their daughter, Kezia, for baptism, but she did not live long, and was buried on September 22. Then came John in 1817, followed by Jacob in 1821. Jacob only lived seven months. Turkey Court cannot have been a healthy place to live, and the Bustons probably could not afford to call in the doctor.

Fishmonger, bricklayer, innkeeper, soldier, weaver, mason, labourer, silk-weaver and carpenter—all these occupations can be found in Wilton by looking at the parish registers after 1813. The parish was clearly a busy place, and the registers a very fruitful source.

The other source already mentioned in this section and also earlier in the book comprises the account books of the church-wardens. The accounts for the year 1714–15 are printed earlier in the book, and some ideas are there set out for suggested topics for study. One topic only briefly mentioned was the church band; and here are some of the entries on the subject, which are, by themselves, a kind of history of music in Wilton church over the past century and a half:

June 21st 1728. Received of Joan Street widow for the corner seat in the middle alley in the parish church heretofore the singers seat for the term of three lives.

In 1773 a gallery was built for the singers, probably in the tower, and five "singing books" and a pitch pipe were provided for their use. They sang, you see, unaccompanied, the church had no organ or piano. In 1801 a 'cello was bought, and later a violin and a double bass, but strings for them were costly:

1801	Paid for Violoncello & case for ditto	£4	5s.	2d.
	Strings for the violincello		7s.	2d.
1802	Strings for the violincello		5s.	0d.
1806	Strings for violincello & violin for two years	£1	10s.	0d.

1808	For strings for violin & violincello	£2	5s.	0d.
1810	Strings for Bass Viol		10s.	0d.
1811	Bag for violincello		5s.	0d.
	Strings for ditto etc.		15s.	0d.
1812	William Turle for Hairing the Bass Bow		2s.	6d.
1814	Paid for strings etc. omitted last account		15s.	0d.
	Paid for strings		10s.	0d.

From 1815 until 1842 the churchwardens made regular payments to the singers, sometimes called "instrument money"; this seems to have been designed to cover the costs of the maintenance of their instruments. This church band was replaced in 1842 by an organ, paid for by public subscription, and money was paid to "Summerhays, organist". Mr. Summerhays was the bandmaster of the West Somerset Yeomanry Cavalry. It seems as if the organ was not quite satisfactory, for "string money" was paid to the band again in the next year, and the organist left in 1846. The organ was regularly tuned, but "string money" was paid until 1853. By 1880 there was a choir in the church, and the choirboys were paid £9 a year between them. The organist himself, Mr. Frost, had a salary of £4, plus three guineas for repairing and tuning the organ; and by 1902 the organ blower was being paid £2 a year to keep the organ going.

Transport
Wilton, as we have seen from the maps of the parish, had no canal or railway running through it; but one of its roads, leading from Taunton to Trull, and finally to Honiton in Devon, was under the care of local turnpike trustees. When the bad state of the roads around Taunton eventually led to an Act of Parliament in 1752 allowing a group of men to take tolls on certain roads in the area in order to pay for their proper repair, this road through Wilton was mentioned:

Whereas [runs the Act] . . . the highways leading from the New Angel in Taunton aforesaid through the Parishes of Wilton, Trull and Pitminster . . . to . . . Churchtaunton in the County of Devon . . . are become so ruinous and bad (in the Winter Season) that the same cannot, by the ordinary course appointed by the Laws and Statutes of this Realm [i.e. by the parish waywardens], be sufficiently repaired and amended. . . . That for the better surveying, ordering, repairing, and keeping in Repair, the said several Highways or Roads, it shall be in the Power of the Right Honourable John Earl of Egmont [and other gentlemen named] . . . who are hereby nominated and appointed Trustees . . . to erect, or cause to be erected, a Gate or Gates, Turnpike or Turnpikes, in, upon, or cross, and Part or Parts of the said Highways or Roads, and to demand, receive, and take the Tolls and Duties following. . . . [there follow a list of charges similar to those on pp. 57–8. See plate 15 for the remains of the board of charges formerly on the wall of the Shuttern Tollhouse, now in the County Museum at Taunton.]

As a result of this Act of Parliament, the Taunton Turnpike Trust was formed and their records, covering the period 1752 to 1876, are now available for study in the County Record Office at Taunton. At one time these records, as we shall see, were actually kept in one of the tollhouses. From them information can be obtained on many aspects of the Trust's work: you can discover how new roads were made, bridges built, pavements constructed. Here we shall trace the histories of two tollhouses, both just outside the parish, but both built to collect tolls from those travelling on the road running through it.

The story of these two houses can be built up by searching the Minute Books of the Trust which record the decisions taken by the turnpike trustees at their monthly meetings:

Shuttern Tollhouse (plate 14)

5 May 1752   Ordered that Three Capital Gate to be erected . . . one near the road leading to Hillbishopps . . . the Gate Keepers at each of the said Gates have a salary payable by the Treasurer of fiveteen pounds per annum.

7 May 1752   William Heath appointed first keeper.

5 Dec. 1752   A lamp was set up by the gate.

The gate was soon succeeded by a tollhouse, though exactly where it stood we do not know. In 1815 the Trustees decided to build a new house:

6 June 1815   Ordered that a new Toll house be erected in lieu of the present Toll house at Shuttern Gate . . . at an expense not exceeding four hundred pounds. . . .

This had been completed by May 14, 1816, when it was "ordered that the garden behind the Shuttern Toll house be enclosed and that a pump be therein erected and a Necessary built and also that a shed be erected in front of the house . . ." It was still being paid for in September, when George Pollard was paid £30 "in respect of the stone cornice at the new Toll house at Shuttern".

This tollhouse, as the addition of a cornice implies, was a more substantial building than most of its kind. It is not recognised as a tollhouse by most people today, since its shape makes it more like a private house. The reason is partly because it was regarded in some way as the Headquarters of the Taunton Turnpike Trustees who, in 1820 (minute of February 1) "ordered that a place of security, Fire Proof, be made at the Shuttern Toll house for depositing the Muniments and papers relating to the Trust...." But although in shape it does not look like most tollhouses, its position, shown on the map of 1821 (plate 3), corresponds exactly with its position today. George Pollard's cornice can still clearly be seen.

About 1840 a new road, still today called the Wellington New Road, was constructed, beginning half a mile west of the Shuttern tollhouse:

3 May 1841   Order to discontinue on or before 29 Sept. next Shuttern Toll gate and toll gates be erected in lieu one where the new road begins, another at or near Wild Oak on the N. side and also a bar or side gate at a place called Whitley Cross. [This order was revoked at a meeting on 9 July.]

Eventually, however, ten years later, this plan was put into effect, and the history of the tollhouse is told in the minutes:

3 Dec. 1850   Insured for £200.
5 Aug. 1851   Side bar erected at Whitley Cross.
7 Oct. 1851   "Late" Shuttern tollhouse mentioned. It had therefore been closed.
7 June 1853   Question of selling the tollhouse arose. The records kept there were transferred to 4 Hammet Street.
5 July 1853   Trustees decide to sell.
2 Aug. 1853   Offered to Miss Norman of Wilton Lodge (see p. 104) next door. She refused to buy.
6 Sept. 1853   Sold to Mrs. Hannah Stark, widow, for £400.

Wheatley Tollhouse (plate 16)
Closely connected with the Shuttern tollhouse, was that at Wheatleigh, also just over the parish boundary at the top of the narrow lane called Hovelands Lane, leading from Galmington. A side gate, as we have seen, was erected here in 1851, to collect tolls from travellers who might think to miss the new gates along the Wellington New Road by making this detour. In May 1857

the Trustees agreed to advertise for tenders to erect a tollhouse on the spot. John Spiller agreed to do the work for £55, and his tender was accepted (minute of May 5). In 1872, when the turnpike trust was about to be wound up, the house was valued at £70, and two years later (minute June 2, 1874) it was sold to Mr. Sibley for £100. The house stood until about 1963, when the road was widened to serve the new houses in the Galmington area.

We should not forget, in our interest in tollhouses, that roads were the main concern of the turnpike trustees, and that the houses were only built to allow for convenient collection of tolls to finance road repairs and development. Few specific references to roads in Wilton have been found in the trustees' minutes, though there are at least two entries to show that improvements were certainly made, and one that payment of tolls was on occasions unpopular:

1 Aug. 1826   Order that a Committee ... be appointed to view the road between Mrs. Cliffe's rails and Whitley's Cross. ....

26 Aug. 1826   [Decision that this stretch of road be widened at a cost not exceeding £45. Part of this stretch can be seen in plate 15].

19 Mar. 1816   Ordered that the Clerk do apply to Henry Pring in consequence of a complaint this day made by Edward Blandy of his having forced open the Turnpike Gate at Shuttern. ....

The Parish of Wilton in the Nineteenth Century

As we saw in the second section, Wilton was beginning to be the home of prosperous people by the end of the seventeenth century. This movement must have continued in the following hundred and fifty years, and by the end of the nineteenth century many of Taunton's professional men, lawyers and bankers and solicitors as well as gentlemen of independent means, were building themselves houses there. But there were still farms in the parish, and another feature was the development of industrial housing and of market gardening.

The sources used to study these particular developments here are parish rate books, now at the County Record Office, which cover the period 1836–1867 (with a number of gaps), and the *Post Office Directories* of 1859, 1861, 1866 and 1875, unless otherwise stated. Directories were issued at intervals until 1939 and sometimes later, but this small selection will indicate how they can be used.

There were a number of factories in nineteenth-century Taunton, and those with an eye to business might do well by providing small houses for the workers. Thomas Burton was one of these. In the earliest rate book (1836) he is found as owner of three dwellings called Moneymash Cottage, fifteen houses in Turkey Court, and ten in a street named after himself, Burton Place. The name Turkey Court came about because of the "drugget" or coarse floor covering called Turkey, then manufactured in the town. (A local tradition also derives it from its position close to the gaol, as Turnkey Court.) Burton Place still survives, at that point in the parish nearest the town and most convenient for the workers who lived there.

The inhabitants of these small houses were of no concern to the compilers of Directories. They were not "clergy and gentry", nor were they "commercial", the only two categories the compilers recognised! But from 1861 until 1875 the following craftsmen and businessmen occur:

Arbery, Isaac, boot and shoemaker, Wilton St.	1861–75
Coleman, Mrs. Sarah, shopkeeper, Galmington	1861
Cousins, William, seedsman & market gardener, Sherford	1866–75
France, John, shoemaker, Galmington	1875
Gould, Henry, shoemaker, Galmington	1875
Grigg, William, grocer, Sherford	1861
Nash, Benjamin, market gardener, Wilton	1861–75
Proctor, Mrs. Louisa Fanny, laundress, Wilton St.	1866
Quick, James, market gardener, Sherford	1866
Rowe, George, gardener, Wilton	1861–6
Southwood, Thomas Charles, baker, tallow chandler, Galmington	1866–75
Tarrington, Henry, market gardener, Wilton	1861
Thomas, William, seedsman & market gardener, Wilton St.	1866–75
Wyatt, William, hollow wood turner, Sherford	1866–75

From the Directories we can also trace the farms which were once in the parish:

Cutler's, now Cutliffe, Farm: William Perrin, farmer, 1861–75
Poole Farm: Thomas Taylor, farmer, 1861–6
                Vincent Taylor, 1875
Pack's Farm, Sherford: John Langford, farmer, 1861–75

Other farmers in 1861 included William Rose at Sherford Farm,

William Winter, farmer and tanner in Sherford, and Mrs. Joanna Wyatt, of Tripp's Farm, also in Sherford. Sherford, like Galmington, was a small hamlet surrounded by open country, and farming was naturally the main occupation who lived there.

But most people in the parish lived in Wilton itself, and there, in the large private houses surrounded by their own extensive grounds such as Wheatleigh Lodge, Highlands, and Hovelands Lodge, and in the newly-developed properties of Haines Hill (see below), lived solicitors, bankers, retired service officers and clergy. A search in the *Directory* for 1861 produced the following list:

Badcock, Henry, JP, Wheatleigh Lodge, banker
*Bastard, Revd. Henry H., Windsor, Haines Hill, clergyman
Beadon, Edwards, Highlands, solicitor
*Carver, Richard, Haines Hill, architect (see p. 94)
Doveton, Capt. Frederick, JP, Woodville, Haines Hill, retired
service officer

French, Henry, BA, Haines Hill, schoolmaster
*Griffith, Revd. W. H., Wilton Lodge, headmaster
Kinglake, Hamilton, Wilton House, surgeon
*Parr, Capt. Frederick, Haines Hill, retired service officer
*Sibly, Thomas, BA, Haines Hill, headmaster
*Spencer, Revd. John W., BA, The Lodge, vicar of Wilton
*Winsloe, Lieut. Richard, Haines Hill, retired service officer
Woodland, William, Haines Hill, solicitor.

By 1875 those marked with an asterisk were no longer living in the parish, but the following had moved in:

Badcock, Henry J., Hovelands Lodge, banker
Channing, Henry, Bath House, solicitor
Coles, James Bond, 7 Haines Hill, solicitor
Kite, George H., 6 Haines Hill, solicitor
Maynard, Walter, Fons George, estate agent
Trenchard, Montague, Haines Hill, solicitor.

So the parish was the home in 1875 of five of the town's leading solicitors and two bankers, as well as of farmers, market gardeners and factory workers. But it is the gentry who, through their houses, have left such a mark on the parish; and so "biographies" of a road and two houses follow, to show how rate books and Directories can be used for more detailed work, and also to illustrate the value of studies of individual areas within a parish where work on a wider scale would be difficult,

Until 1845 there were three fields in the parish, lying together, called respectively Haines's Six, Five and Five Acres. In 1840, according to the tithe map at the County Record Office, they were owned by the Rev. William Rawlins, and were farmed by Isaac Small of Sherford. Until April 1845 the rates were paid as usual and the property was naturally described as "land"; but in that month the two five-acre fields were divided into 9 plots, and in July were described as "building land". In October there were 9 "houses" and two "plots", but work had not finished even on the houses, for only three were completed by January 1846. In October 1846 12 houses were rated (but still not necessarily finished) and one plot was still vacant. In January 1847 11 houses seem to have been occupied. The name by which the road is still known, Haines Hill, was first given in October 1845.

This was a high-class housing development, built for the gentry (plate 17). By 1859 (according to a Directory), six were occupied by people in the "clergy and gentry" section, and two others by an architect and a solicitor. By 1875 there were seventeen such occupants, including four solicitors, a clergyman, two service officers, and a boys' preparatory school. Today some of the houses have been divided, and some of the large plots are occupied by modern dwellings built in the grounds of the earlier houses, but the road has not greatly changed in character, a number of brass plates testifying to the presence of doctors and surgeons.

From the same sources let us now trace the histories in the period 1836–75 of two houses in the parish, Wilton Lodge and Belmont (plates 18 and 19).

(a) A house now known as Wilton Lodge was first so called in the rate books in October 1854. In the same books it can be traced through its owner, a Miss Norman, back to her father, Samuel Norman, who called it Wilton Place in 1842, and who was holding it in 1836 when the series of rate books begins. From 1854, with rate books and Directories it can be traced by its present name, and its history during our period may be tabulated thus:

Date	Name	Owner	Occupier
1836–42	—	Samuel Norman	Samuel Norman
1842–45	Wilton Place	,, ,,	,, ,,
1845–47	,, ,,	Executors of S.N.	Executors of S.N.
1847	,, ,,	,, ,,	House empty

By April 1849						
–July 1849	„	„	Miss Anne Norman			Charles Collis
October 1849	„	„	„	„	„	Mrs. Collis
October 1854						
–1857	Wilton Lodge	„	„	„		Miss Culverwell
1857–59	„	„	„	„	„	Edward Cobb
1859–67	„	„	„	„	„	Revd. William Griffith (head of Independent School, now Taunton School)
1875	„	„	?			Mrs. Eliza Meynier (nee Griffith), ladies' boarding school.

(b) The other house is much larger. Its ownership can be traced in a similar way, but its history is of significance for another reason. It was once surrounded by extensive grounds open to the public. These grounds have now been whittled away by successive waves of building, but the trees which a hundred years ago made it famous still stand to give that part of the parish an individual character (see plate 19). The house is called Belmont, and stands on a hill commanding extensive views. Its grounds once occupied both sides of the turnpike road to Trull. The *Post Office Directory* of 1875 thus describes it:

Belmont and Mount Nebo are the property and residence of John Marshall esquire: the grounds lie on each side of the road at Wilton, and are tastefully planted with shrubs and evergreens, including the Wellingtonia Gigantea and Cryptomeria Elegans, which here grow luxuriantly: the aviary, erected at a cost of £800, contains a rare selection of birds: the fernery was designed by Black, at a cost of £950, and comprises upwards of 350 varieties of ferns, all hardy: the orchid house contains plants of exceptional interest, including the very rare Masdevallia Trochilus (here in full bloom), with the varieties Harryana and Veitchii, also the Dendrobium Wardianum, and other very choice plants: the public are admitted to these grounds at all reasonable times.

The grounds were still open in 1889 (*Kelly's Directory*), but the Mount Nebo section was offered for sale as 22 building plots in 1892 (*Somerset County Gazette*, March 26), and a new road, called Mount Nebo, was cut through the gardens. Only three plots were sold immediately (*County Gazette*, April 2), and building continued there until after the Second World War. The main part of the Belmont Grounds was divided in 1904 (Sale

Catalogue in the possession of the *County Archaeological Society*). The plan of the grounds which accompanies the catalogue includes many statues and the "Temple", "used as a summer House or Study, highly decorated at great cost", but no trace of the aviary or fernery. The grounds immediately around the house are now occupied by modern houses which still allow the mansion to retain its former grandeur.

So Wilton has become, in the nineteenth century, principally a parish for the well-to-do. There are workers, there are farmers, there are market gardeners; but the rate books and the Directories show clearly that Wilton has become the home of the wealthy.

BOOK LIST

As suggested in the Introduction you should ask your local librarian for help in finding any books written about your town or village. You will also have discovered from your visits to your local County Record Office what other sources are available beyond those described in this book. The following general books on local history may prove useful:

MAPS
J. B. Harley, *Maps for the Local Historian: a Guide to the British Sources* (National Council for Social Service, 1972).

ARCHAEOLOGY
P. J. Fowler (ed.), *Archaeology and the Landscape* (John Baker, 1972).
Field Archaeology; some notes for beginners (Ordnance Survey, 1947).

LANDSCAPE AND FIELDWORK
M. Beresford, *History on the Ground* (Methuen, reprinted 1972).
W. G. Hoskins, *Fieldwork in Local History* (Faber, 1967); *History from the Farm* (ed.) (Faber, 1970); *Local History in England* (Longmans, 1959); *The Making of the English Landscape* (Penguin Books, 1970).
Hedges and Local History (National Council for Social Service, 1971).

PLACE AND FIELD NAMES
E. Ekwall, *Dictionary of English Place-Names* (Oxford, 4th edition, 1960).
John Field, *English Field Names; a dictionary* (David and Charles, 1972).

BUILDINGS
M. W. Barley, *The English Farmhouse and Cottage* (R.K.P., 1961).
N. Harvey, *The Story of Farm Buildings* (Young Farmers Club Booklet 27, Evans Bros., 1953).

INDUSTRIAL ARCHAEOLOGY
Charles Hadfield, *British Canals* (David and Charles, 1973).
K. Hudson, *Industrial Archaeology* (John Baker, 1963).
Industrial Archaeology (periodical, David and Charles).

PARISH AND OTHER LOCAL RECORDS
W. E. Tate, *The Parish Chest* (3rd edition, 1969).
J. West, *Village Records* (Macmillan, 1962).

Index

Abbotsbury, Dorset, 42
account rolls, 29; town accounts, 65
Act of Parliament, 5, 57, 61, 63–4,
    98–9
advertisements, 69–70
aerial photographs, 8, 21–2; and see
    camera, photographs
Anglo-Saxon Chronicle, 24–5
apprentices, 55, 65
arable, 7; and see fields, strips
Archaeological Society, xiv, 22–3, 106
archaeologist, 2, 20–1; archaeology,
    xiv, 23, 107
archdeacon, 53
archivist, xiii, 22, 30, 41, 74, 87
armour, 45
arms, coat of, 45, 94–5

bailey, 20; and see castle
Bath, Somerset, 27
Bath and Wells, Bishop of, 87
beacons, 2
beadle, 26
beggars, 47
bells, 46, 52, 54; and see ringers
Berkley, Somerset, 47–8
Birmingham, 25–6
bishop, 24, 53
Bishop's Lydeard, Somerset, 45
Blome, Richard, mapmaker, 1
boats, see ships
Boatswain family, 43
books, 89
bordars, 25
botany, 9
boundaries, 7, 11–15, 81–3; boundary
    marks, 3, 11–12, 22, 54; boundary
    stones, 14
bounds, beating the, 11
brass mills, 36

brasses, see memorials
bridges, 2, 17–18, 22, 83, 86, 99;
    fig. IV, V; pl. 5
bridleways, 22
British Transport Commission, 60
Bronze Age, 83–4
building materials, 32; brick, 34, 37,
    39, 84; plaster, 32, 37, 39, 92;
    stone, 4, 9, 33–4, 42, 62; timber,
    32–3, 37, 39; wattle and daub, 32
building plots, 104–5
burials, 2, 20
Burton, Thomas, 94, 102; family, 97
buses, 64
business houses, 67

camera, 17, 35; and see photography
canal, 4, 57, 60–4, 66–7, 77, 98
Carver, Richard, architect, 94, 103
castle, 2, 8, 20, 34
census, 85
church, 2, 14, 26, 33, 42–55, 76, 82,
    86, 93–8; music, 54, 98; rate, 28,
    51–3, 80; services, 53–4; yard, 42,
    53, 94
churchwardens, 46, 51–2, 71, 80, 98;
    accounts, 51–5, 94, 97, pl. 1
cloth, 28, 63
coach, 2, 57, 59, 64, 66–7
coal, 18–19, 61; and see wharf
common, 5–7
council, 22, 71, 74
court roll, 29
crops, see farm produce
Curry Mallet, Somerset, 26–8

dairying, 76, 93
deerparks, 8, 15, 19, fig. II
deposited plans, 60–1, 63–4
dialect, 41

109